P9-CRK-864

DIAL M

DIAL M

William Swan [signature]

WILLIAM SWANSON

The Murder of Carol Thompson

**BOREALIS
BOOKS**

Borealis Books is an imprint of the Minnesota
Historical Society Press.

www.borealisbooks.org

© 2006 by William Swanson. All rights reserved.
No part of this book may be used or reproduced
in any manner whatsoever without written permission except in the case of brief quotations em-
bodied in critical articles and reviews. For information, write to Borealis Books, 345 Kellogg Blvd.
W., St. Paul, MN 55102-1906.

The Minnesota Historical Society Press is a member of the Association of American University
Presses.

Manufactured in the United States of America

10 9 8 7 6 5 4 3 2 1

∞ The paper used in this publication meets the
minimum requirements of the American National
Standard for Information Sciences—Permanence
for Printed Library Materials, ANSI Z39.48-1984.

International Standard Book Number
ISBN 13: 978-0-87351-587-0 (paper)
ISBN 10: 0-87351-587-0 (paper)

Library of Congress
Cataloging-in-Publication Data

Swanson, William, 1945-
Dial M : the murder of Carol Thompson
  / William Swanson.
    p.   cm.
  ISBN 0-87351-560-9 (cloth : alk. paper)
  1. Thompson, Carol, 1928 or 9-1963.
  2. Murder victims—Minnesota—Saint Paul—
  Case studies.
  3. Murder—Minnesota—Saint Paul—
  Case studies.
  I. Title.

HV6534.S193S92 2006
364.152'309776581—dc22   2005029864

To Libby

Murder is mysterious; even if we know all the who-what-when facts ..., the distance between our own lives and the act of murder leaves a space where mystery creeps in....

[A murder story] is about what must be imagined, what can't actually be seen—what can't, in any verifiable way, be known. Even when the murder story involves the solution of a mystery, that solution can't resolve all our questions.

- WENDY LESSER
 Pictures at an Execution: An Inquiry into the Subject of Murder

Murder cases are generally of interest to the extent that they suggest some anomaly or lesson in the world revealed.

- JOAN DIDION
 "L.A. Noir"

Dial M

Photographs follow page 101

AUTHOR'S NOTE

Most factual accounts of murder—including American classics
such as *In Cold Blood* and *The Executioner's Song*—are stories about
murderers. There is nothing mysterious about that. Murderers, after all, usually outlive their victims, and often, thanks to long and
highly publicized investigations, trials, and appeals, they remain
walking, talking public presences years after memories of the victims and the particulars of the murders themselves have faded in
our minds.

The account that follows is different. To be sure, it is a story
about a murder and murderers, perhaps the most infamous murder and murderers in Minnesota history. But it is also very much
about the victims: the literal victim—a thirty-four-year-old wife
and mother who was fatally beaten and stabbed in her St. Paul

home on March 6, 1963—and her four children, ages six to thirteen at the time of her death, who have grown into adulthood and middle age beneath the long arc of that horrible crime. The fact that, in this case, the husband and father of the victims was judged responsible for the murder makes it impossible to think about, much less tell, one story without the other.

This, then, is both a family saga and a true account of a notorious crime. And happily—granted, an unlikely word given the circumstances—the saga does not end when the book does.

DIAL M

PART ONE

Cotton and Carol

Some people have expected to see his crimes written in the face of
a murderer, and have been disappointed because they did not, as
if this impeached the distinction between virtue and vice.

- WILLIAM HAZLITT
  "On Cant and Hypocrisy"

The Scene of a Cutting

1.

Moments after nine o'clock on Wednesday morning, March 6, 1963, Mrs. Fritz Pearson, a physician's wife who lived at 1707 Hill-crest Avenue in the Highland Park neighborhood of St. Paul, Minnesota, glanced out her living room window and saw a most unusual sight.

She saw a woman slumped on the front steps of the Tyler Neptune house directly across the street. The woman, Mrs. Pearson later told the police, appeared to be "almost nude," draped in only a light blue coat or wrap of some kind. Moreover, despite the weather—the temperature was hovering near freezing and a light snow was falling—the woman seemed to be barefoot. More puzzling yet, her face and upper body looked as though they were covered with blood. Then, as Mrs. Pearson and a hired man who was painting the Pearsons' living room watched, the woman struggled to her feet and staggered across the yard to the Harry Nelson home next door.

When the doorbell rang at 1700 Hillcrest, Mrs. Harry Nelson was in the breakfast nook off the kitchen, listening to the nine o'clock news. Opening the front door, she was astonished to find a bloodied, barefoot woman wrapped in a light blue bathrobe shivering in the snow. The woman was clutching her throat, though it appeared that most of the blood was coming from wounds on her scalp and face. "I thought it looked like she was burned, but it was blood," Mrs. Nelson said later.

"Help me," Mrs. Nelson thought the woman said. "Help me." The woman's voice was faint, a forced whisper, and her words were difficult to understand.

Mrs. Nelson, her husband, and an adult son who had also been in the kitchen brought the woman into the house and laid her down on a rug inside the front door. Despite her difficulty speaking, the woman managed to tell them that there was a knife in her throat. One of the Nelsons asked who had done this to her, and in a faint voice, she said, "A man did it." When Mrs. Nelson asked her name, the woman's answer was unintelligible. "Johnson," she seemed to be saying. Mr. Nelson called the police.

Within seconds, Dr. Fritz Pearson, who had been alerted by his wife, crossed the street to the Nelsons' house and began attending to the injured woman. With towels and washcloths provided by Ruth Nelson, the elderly physician carefully wiped enough blood off the woman's face for them to see who it was. No less astonishing than her appearance at the front door was the woman's identity.

It was, of all people, their neighbor Carol Thompson.

2.

At 9:07, Archie Hines, the dispatcher on duty at the Public Safety Building on East Eleventh Street in downtown St. Paul, responded to a call from a Mr. Harry Nelson in Highland Park and directed Squad 302, a police ambulance, to 1700 Hillcrest Avenue. A "badly injured lady" was how Hines, in his departmental report, described the objective of the police response.

Squad 302, manned by Officers Harry Hughley and Willard La-Bathe, picked up the dispatcher's call near the intersection of Selby and Snelling, slightly more than two miles from the Highland Park address. But the light snowfall that had begun a couple of hours earlier had slicked the streets and slowed the morning's traffic, so Sergeants John Mercado and Roy Shepard, who had heard Hines's call in their squad car a few blocks from the scene, arrived on Hillcrest first. In *his* report, filed later that morning, Mercado said that he and Shepard found a woman lying on the floor of the Nelsons' house, bleeding from wounds in her neck and right eye. "[The] wounds were small and appeared to be stab wounds," he wrote.

While Dr. Pearson administered first aid, Mercado asked the woman if she could tell him who had assaulted her. Struggling for breath, she was unable to answer. Mrs. Nelson told the officers that the woman's name was Carol Ann Thompson and that Carol, her husband, T. Eugene Thompson, and their four children lived three houses down the block.

When the ambulance arrived a few minutes later, Mercado directed Hughley and LaBathe inside the house with a stretcher. Later that day, Hughley wrote: "A woman was lying on her back just to the right of the front door, on the floor, in the dining room. She was clothed in a blue robe which was heavily stained with blood. . . . We observed that the woman had numerous wounds about the forehead, a wound bleeding quite heavily in the right eye, [and] three or four wounds in the neck on the left and right sides. [We also] noticed a shiny metal tip of what appeared to be a knife blade protruding from the left side of the neck."

Hughley and LaBathe carried Carol Thompson to the ambulance and, with red light flashing and siren keening, began the drive to Ancker Hospital, about three and a half miles—on a good day, less than ten minutes—away. While LaBathe negotiated the slippery streets, Hughley, bending over the injured woman, tried to ascertain what had happened back on Hillcrest. But the woman could only shake her head. "She was not receptive to any questions and appeared to be semi-conscious," Hughley said later.

Approaching the hospital's emergency entrance, LaBathe asked dispatcher Hines to tell the medical staff to be ready for an urgent case. "We have a bad one," LaBathe said.

3.

When the ambulance carrying Carol Thompson pulled away from 1700 Hillcrest, Mercado and Shepard jogged down the block to 1720, a two-and-a-half-story brick Tudor four doors from the corner. On the snow-covered brick walkway that led from the public sidewalk, the officers saw footprints coming from the front steps. The storm door was closed, but the inner door was ajar.

Mercado climbed the steps, opened the storm door, and peered into the house. He saw a pool of blood just inside the door. Lying in the blood was a "live shell, caliber unknown" and the "handle of what appeared to be a knife," he reported later that day. He told Shepard to cover the rear of the house while he went back to their car and radioed for help. A second squad arrived within moments, and now four uniformed officers stood guard outside the house, waiting, as prescribed by department policy, for an investigator to arrive before going inside.

Back at 1700, Harry and Ruth Nelson's son, Sidney, had called T. Eugene Thompson, Carol's husband, at his law office downtown. Though he was not a close friend, Sidney, at thirty-three, was roughly Thompson's age and had been a neighbor for five years. "Cotton," he said, using Thompson's nickname, "I don't want to alarm you, but Carol just came to our door, and there appears to have been an accident. Dr. Pearson is with her now." He said an ambulance had arrived and would take Carol to Ancker Hospital. Thompson, Sidney later told police, sounded stunned, but had his wits sufficiently about him to ask the neighbor to call Carol's friend Marjorie Young, who was a nurse, and ask her to go to the hospital.

Instead of going to the nearby hospital himself, Thompson and another lawyer, Donald Kelly, with whom he shared an office suite in the Minnesota Building on West Fourth Street, drove directly to Highland Park, ten minutes away. Thompson stopped briefly at the Nelsons', then proceeded down the block to his home. The officers at the site told him he could not go inside. He did not argue. He and Kelly drove to the hospital, where they arrived about fifteen minutes after the ambulance had brought Carol Thompson to the emergency entrance. Thompson told Officer Hughley that his wife had been in a "good frame of mind" when he and their four children had eaten breakfast and left the house shortly after eight, and that he knew of no one who "might have anything against his wife, his family, or himself."

A few minutes later, Thompson told Detective Robert LaBathe that after leaving the house that morning he had dropped their thirteen-year-old son, Jeffrey, at St. Paul Academy on Randolph Avenue, about a five-minute drive from home. From there, he had continued downtown, to his office on Fourth Street. At about eight-twenty-five or eight-thirty, he told Detective LaBathe, he had called his wife to confirm his plans to look after the kids so Carol could attend a night-school class that evening. "Mrs. Thompson answered the phone and was all right at the time," La-

Bathe reported, paraphrasing Thompson in his report later that day.

In the emergency room, Carol Thompson was fighting for her life. As the medical staff struggled to stabilize her condition, Dr. Ramon Mendiola, Jr., a resident surgeon from the Philippines who was one of the first physicians to see the victim upon her arrival, removed the broken three-inch blade of a stainless steel paring knife from her throat. "She was so pale," Mendiola would testify later. "Her hair was matted with blood, and I couldn't feel her pulse."

Several months later, shown a studio photo of the victim, Ancker Hospital's chief of surgery, Dr. John Perry, Jr., who supervised the emergency treatment, could not identify her, "because," he said, "the person I saw was badly battered and covered with blood."

4.

Ernest Williams, of the St. Paul Police Department's homicide division, was the first detective to arrive at 1720 Hillcrest, at about nine-thirty that morning. A seasoned investigator who had served in both World War II and Korea, Williams led Mercado and Officer Roy LaBell into the silent house. The officers moved cautiously, opening doors, peering around corners, checking behind furniture. The odds were slight that the person or persons who had attacked Carol Thompson would still be in the house, but the officers' training, experience, and common sense demanded a deliberate approach.

On the first floor, Williams and Mercado noted large blood stains and signs of a struggle near the front door and blood smears on and near a kitchen drawer. According to Williams's initial report, the master bedroom on the second floor had been ransacked. Drawers had been pulled out of a dresser and their contents strewn on the floor. The unmade double bed was rumpled. A newspaper, a pair of eyeglasses, and a reading lamp were lying on the bed. The radio on a bedside table was playing softly.

In the second-floor hallway, between the master bedroom and the bathroom at the head of the stairs, lay a pillow. In the bathroom, the tub contained several inches of lukewarm water, and there were "red smears" around the washbasin taps. The other two bedrooms on the second floor and the single bedroom on the third floor both appeared to be undisturbed. A check of the basement revealed nothing amiss there, either.

At one point, the telephone on the kitchen wall rang, shattering the silence. When Williams picked it up, a woman asked for Carol. It was a friend who was unaware of what had happened less than an hour earlier. The detective identified himself and told the caller that Carol was in the hospital.

Outside, additional investigators were arriving in unmarked cars, directed there, in the words of Detective Dan McLaughlin, "to assist at the scene of a cutting." The detectives had come from all over St. Paul—from homes and coffee shops and their cluttered desks in the Public Safety Building downtown—on the orders of the department's homicide commander, Detective Lieutenant George Barkley, and, doubtless, because they were curious. In 1963, home invasions and murderous assaults such as this were highly unusual anywhere in St. Paul, which averaged scarcely a half-dozen murders a year during the early 1960s, but would have been especially freakish in Highland Park, a stable, upper-middle-class corner of the city where the police were rarely called except for an occasional bicycle theft or loud car. Since the end of World War II, Highland Park had been the scene of four separate homicides, including those of three apparently unrelated women and, most recently, in 1960, a fifty-eight-year-old man described in news accounts as a "former pinball machine operator"; still, it was a neighborhood where homeowners did not worry about violent crime and routinely left their doors unlocked. Now, large men bundled against the late-winter weather in fedoras, overcoats, and galoshes bent over the footprints on the Thompsons' sidewalk—the first officers at the site had covered the prints with pieces of cardboard to protect them from the falling snow—as neighbors peered at the strange activity from behind drawn drapes and venetian blinds. Other men, newspaper photographers as well as police officers, prowled around the houses with note pads and big Speed Graphic cameras, their flashbulbs creating small blue-white explosions in the snow-flecked light.

The detectives canvassed the homes on both sides of Hillcrest. At 1726, the house immediately to the west of the Thompsons', Mrs. O.A. Bengel told investigators she had seen and heard nothing out of the ordinary that morning. In fact, she said, she had been unaware of the attack until only a few moments earlier, when she was called by a local radio station, where someone had apparently been monitoring the shortwave police calls. At about nine o'clock, Mrs. Bengel said, she had glanced out her second-floor window at the west window of the Thompsons' master bedroom only a few feet away and thought about calling Carol for coffee; then, for no particular reason, she decided not to. She told the detectives she had seen no one in the Thompsons' window, or in the yard or street below.

Moving westward down the block, one house at a time, the detectives learned of nothing out of the ordinary that morning. Between eight and nine o'clock, as on most weekday mornings, husbands had left their homes for their offices, children walked off to school, and milkmen made their doorstep deliveries. One woman said she had left her house shortly after nine o'clock to run an errand. She had driven up the alley past the Thompsons' garage, but noticed nothing unusual. At several homes, the officers' knocks were unanswered, as entire families had already set out for the day's activities—or the householders inside were unwilling to open the door to unfamiliar callers. At the others the responses were the same:

"Nothing unusual or suspicious noted."

"Saw or heard nothing."

The police department's crime lab staff arrived at the site at about ten-thirty. Williams directed criminalist Theodore Elzerman's attention to the footprints on the snowy sidewalk. The prints were apparently made by a man's shoe in a "rubber with a cross-hatched pattern." A red stain was visible in the pattern of one of the prints.

Elzerman and two assistants then traced the erratic path taken by Carol Thompson en route to the Nelsons' home, three houses to the east. Following her footprints in the snow, the investigators ascertained that the victim had emerged from the side door of her house, run behind the Harold Erikson home next door, passed between the Eriksons' and the Neptunes' houses to the front stoop of the latter (where Mrs. Pearson and the house painter had first spotted her from across the street), then proceeded to the front door of the Nelsons' house at the corner. "Some red staining" was noted at both the rear and front doors of the Eriksons' and Neptunes', indicating that Mrs. Thompson had pounded on the door or rung the bell at both houses. Mrs. Erikson told police she had been upstairs making beds and thought she heard someone at the door, but, assuming it was only the milkman, she had not bothered to answer. Mrs. Neptune was also at home, but said she had heard or seen nothing peculiar around the time in question.

In addition, the investigators discovered "red droplets" on the ground between the neighbors' houses, and "brush-type marks" at the northwest corner of 1706 Hillcrest, "where [the] victim probably touched or leaned against [the house]."

5.

Part of the orderly grid of residential streets that make up the northern half of the neighborhood, Hillcrest Avenue runs straight as an arrow and slightly downhill from Highland Park Golf Course on the east toward the wooded bluffs above the Mississippi River about a mile away. Many of its houses are two- and three-story stucco or brick variations on a Tudor theme, set back from the street behind wide lawns, fronted by shrubs and hedges, and sheltered by mature trees, including, in the early 1960s, massive American elms more than a half-century old. The setting had the scrubbed and fastidious look of a well-to-do suburb, though Highland Park—which was also the site of a sprawling Ford Motor Company assembly plant and a bustling retail district flanking Ford Parkway, a block north of Hillcrest—had been part of the city proper since the 1920s.

Like most of its neighbors on the long block between Fairview and Davern, 1720 Hillcrest had been built in the late 1920s. It was a two-and-a-half-story, red brick Tudor with a sharply peaked roof and a screened three-season porch. A thick, four-foot-high hedge— leafless and spiky in early March—and a tangle of ivy vines clinging to the exterior walls and chimney lent the place a vaguely English look. There was a wide front yard, a somewhat smaller yard around back, and a detached two-car garage accessible from the alley that ran behind the house between Hillcrest and Bohland Avenue to the south.

Inside, a fireplace dominated the front (north) wall of the living room, which, in February 1963, had been freshly painted and softened with new wall-to-wall carpeting. A soft pastel blue—called robin's egg blue and very popular with decorators and homeowners at the time—gave the living room and adjacent dining area a feminine feel. Upstairs was the master bedroom, two slightly smaller bedrooms that were shared by the three Thompson girls, and the main bath; up another flight of stairs, under the roof, were Jeff Thompson's bedroom and an attic storage area. In the basement, a large "rec room," complete with fireplace, wet bar, television set, sofa, and easy chairs, lay at the foot of a flight of steep, squeaky, carpeted stairs, which descended from just inside the side door. A laundry room and additional storage space filled out the basement.

On March 6, 1963, 1720 Hillcrest had the lived-in but temporarily abandoned look of a house whose occupants were away for the day. Here and there were articles of clothing, a sewing box, the morning newspaper, a library book, a stack of phonograph records, a women's magazine. Photographs taken in the kitchen by Elzerman's crime lab crew showed a small coffee pot plugged into the wall, a skillet with the remains of the family's bacon-and-egg breakfast, and dishes awaiting washing in the sink.

Other, more ominous details were included in the criminalist's report:

- A planter tipped over at the top of the second-floor stairs.
- A woman's flannel nightgown and a bag of hair curlers scattered on the bathroom floor.
- A bath mat bunched up and shoved against the built-in tub, which contained four or five inches of tepid water.
- Red smears "of what appeared to be blood" on the washbasin and—of particular interest to investigators— a length of red rubber hose, an inch thick and about fourteen inches long, that lay on the tiled floor beneath it.
- Blood on several articles of clothing and other items that had been tossed about the master bedroom down the hall— and what appeared to be a piece of a pistol grip.
- Blood smears on the hallway wall near a linen closet.

Despite the evidence of mayhem upstairs, the attack on Carol Thompson had, by all appearances, reached its full fury on the main floor, in the hallway that ran between the front door and the kitchen along the east end of the house. The wall, a closet door, and drapes "bore numerous red stains," according to the criminalist's report, and, in two places, hair fibers adhered to the encrusted blood. In one spot, blood had soaked through the rug onto the hardwood floor. Near the front door, the wooden handle of a small knife lay in the pooled blood. Nearby were three thirty-caliber bullets and fragments of a plastic-laminate pistol grip similar to the piece found upstairs. Under the corner of the bunched-up hall rug, investigators found a woman's white-metal "tea ring" with "a relatively large white stone in the center [and] several small white stones mounted in hearts about the large stone's periphery." Where a safety chain was attached to the frame around the front door, the wood had been pulled away from the wall, and there were traces of plaster and paint on the floor.

In the kitchen, at the other end of the short hallway, a drawer had been yanked open and several knives had been partially pulled out of a knife tray. Both the drawer and the linoleum floor beneath it were spotted with blood. There were also blood smears on the side door.

In a report drafted later that day, the investigators recreated what seemed to be a likely scenario. The assailant apparently first tried to shoot Mrs. Thompson. Failing that, he beat her with his pistol. When the pistol-whipping did not "accomplish his purpose," he "availed himself of a kitchen knife, returned to the hallway, and finished the attack."

6.

The results of the attack were obvious at Ancker Hospital. There, despite the exhaustive efforts of Dr. Perry and his staff, Carol Thompson lay dying.

She had arrived at the hospital unresponsive and without measurable blood pressure. "Two stab wounds were noted in the anterior neck," a pathologist, Dr. Kevin Lawler, wrote in his autopsy report that afternoon. There were, in addition, "numerous stellate lacerations of the scalp from which [Mrs. Thompson] apparently lost a great deal of blood." Her skull had been fractured, and there were multiple cuts and bruises on her scalp, face, and neck. Her hands were cut in several places, including the backs, suggesting that she had fought her attacker and tried to shield her face. There was no evidence that she had been sexually assaulted.

Perry's team worked on Carol Thompson for more than three hours, applying the most up-to-date technology available in critical-care settings. They inserted a tube to help her breathe. When that failed, they performed a tracheotomy. Because the victim's heartbeat was "inadequate or absent," the doctors externally massaged her heart. They drilled a hole in her skull to allow access to a possible hematoma. But their resuscitative efforts were not equal to her injuries, and Carol was pronounced dead at 12:58 PM. She was thirty-four years old.

On her death certificate filed with the Minnesota Department of Health on March 8, Perry described the immediate cause of death as "cardiac arrest due to external hemorrhage due to multiple stab wounds and lacerations of [the] scalp, face, neck, and hands." As to how the victim had incurred those injuries, the death certificate said simply: "Patient beaten and stabbed with knife."

7.

Family members and friends had begun gathering at the Highland Park home of Helen and Harry Zabel, Carol's maternal aunt and her husband, by eleven o'clock that morning. The Zabels lived on Rome Avenue, only a few blocks from the Thompsons. Aside from Otto and Antonia Swoboda, Carol's parents, they were the only close relatives who lived in St. Paul, so their home was a logical place for Carol's loved ones to gather to comfort one another, exchange news, and watch the periodic bulletins and updates on TV.

By one o'clock, the Zabels' home was full of stunned and shaken acquaintances, several of whom had driven to St. Paul from southern Minnesota and Wisconsin. The Thompson children—Jeffrey, thirteen; Patricia, eleven; Margaret, nine; and Amy, six—had been picked up and brought to the house after their mother was taken to the hospital, told only that she had been hurt. Within an hour of her death, the Swobodas and T. Eugene Thompson arrived from the hospital. Thompson sobbed uncontrollably as he gathered his frightened and bewildered children around him.

Thompson had been interviewed a second time at the hospital before Carol died, this time in a physician's office by senior homicide investigator Gerald Bodin. Thompson had reiterated his morning schedule, told the detective that his wife had been wearing a bathrobe over her nightgown when he left for the office, and suggested a possible suspect: a window salesman with whom the Thompsons had done business the previous year and who seemed to have had a crush—unreciprocated, T. Eugene said—on Carol. Thompson told Bodin he would check his files to see if there might be an unhappy client or someone else he knew or had encountered professionally whom the police should check out.

At the Zabels' that afternoon, Detectives Grant Willinger and Fred Buechner, on the instructions of Lieutenant Barkley, asked Thompson if they could talk to his three older children. Thompson said they could and accompanied the kids into a first-floor bedroom, away from the gathering crowd. According to Buechner's report, written later that day, Thompson told his children, "Remember, we discussed this and agreed that after today we will not talk about it again." Thompson, Buechner noted, repeated the remark a short time later.

The detectives talked first to Jeff. The oldest of the four siblings, he may have been the most composed that day, though Buechner's report says nothing about the emotional state of any of the children. Jeff confirmed what Mr. Thompson had told the police at the hospital. He said he had left the house with his father at about eight o'clock that morning and arrived at St. Paul Academy a few minutes later. He usually walked the eight blocks to school, but that day his father had offered him a ride. Probably in response to a question, Jeff said that he never locked the side door when he left the house and always found the side door unlocked when he returned.

Margaret, who called herself Meg, told the detectives that she had been the next to leave the house that morning, about ten minutes after eight. Margaret was a fifth-grader at Highland Park Elementary. She said that she, too, had departed by the side door and left the door unlocked, as she always did. It had been snowing. A girlfriend often met her in the Thompsons' yard, but had not been there that day, so Margaret had walked the three blocks to school by herself.

When it was her turn, Patricia (Patty) said that she and Amy had been the last to leave the house that morning. They followed the same short route that Margaret took to school, leaving a minute or two later by the side door, which they also left unlocked. Patty affirmed Jeff's statement that the door was never locked when someone was home. She also said her mother was either in the kitchen or the living room when she and Amy left for school. Her mother was wearing a bathrobe and pajamas. There was no one in the yard.

After the children were excused, the detectives asked their father a few more questions, beginning with a query about the side door. The Thompson home had no back door. The side door, which faced east and was situated just around the northeast corner of the house from the front entrance, was the door the family used most often, saving wear and tear, Mr. Thompson explained, on the new carpet in the living room. Thompson said the side door could be locked if the "night tumbler" was pushed out, but that the children did not know how the lock worked. The detectives asked if he had used the bathtub before going to work. He said that he had and was certain that he had pulled the drain plug when he finished, though he had not waited to see if all the water had emptied. Asked about the length of rubber hose found in the bathroom, he replied that he used something similar at their lake home, "to siphon out the boat." Whether this was the same piece of hose, he would not know, he said, until he looked at it, and, in any case, he had no idea how the hose the police found had ended up in the bathroom. Maybe it had been dropped there, he suggested, by one of the kids.

The detectives also asked him about the "$4,000 plus" in cash that he had apparently mentioned earlier as having been missing from the house before the murder, and then waited while Donald Kelly retrieved one of Thompson's briefcases from the downtown office suite the two lawyers shared. Forcing open the locked grip with a screwdriver, Thompson pulled out a sealed envelope containing forty-four $100 bills. Describing himself as absentminded, he said he had obviously misplaced the cash, which he said he had taken with him on a gambling trip to Las Vegas the previous fall.

For some reason, the detectives asked Thompson about the morning paper, "and he said he placed it on the hall banister when he left [for work]," Buechner concluded. "He also said that he could not imagine his wife going [anywhere] without her glasses because she is near-sighted."

8.

By mid-afternoon, news of the attack on Carol Thompson, and then of her death, had spread well beyond Ancker Hospital and

Highland Park. Twin Cities television and radio stations, eager to apply their new mobile technology to live, on-site coverage, had crews at both the crime scene and the hospital. Reporters had crowded into the hallway outside George Barkley's homicide headquarters in the Public Safety Building and staked out T. Eugene Thompson's law office in the Minnesota Building. The evening papers in both St. Paul and Minneapolis had sketchy but vivid front-page, above-the-fold reports of the assault on the streets by three o'clock. The *Dispatch*'s inch-high headline declaimed, "Wife of Attorney Stabbed, Killed." The *Star*'s: "St. Paul Mother of 4 Stabbed to Death in Home."

The victim was publicly identified as Carol S. Thompson—the S. standing for Swoboda, her maiden name—and she was immediately and almost invariably from that point forward described as "the wife of a prominent St. Paul attorney." The papers identified her husband as the chairman of the Criminal Law Committee of the Minnesota Bar Association and the village attorney of suburban North St. Paul, and gave the names and ages of the Thompson children.

Both the *St. Paul Dispatch* and the *Minneapolis Star*—the Twin Cities' evening dailies in 1963 (the cities had separate morning and evening papers until the early 1980s)—recounted Mrs. Thompson's barefoot flight to the Nelsons' house, the first aid administered by Dr. Pearson, and the futile attempts by Dr. Perry's emergency room staff to save the woman's life. The *Dispatch* quoted Mrs. Thompson telling Ruth Nelson, "A man did it. . . . He came to the door." In the *Star*, Lieutenant Barkley said the victim, upon answering her front door, was assaulted by a man wielding a blunt object; she was struck on the head several times and left unconscious in the "vestibule." "She later crawled or staggered about 12 feet along a hallway, where she was stabbed with a paring knife," the story continued, paraphrasing Barkley.

The *Dispatch*'s front-page photo displayed footprints, "apparently made by the man who stabbed and beat Mrs. Thompson," in the snow outside 1720 Hillcrest. Other photos on an inside page showed the dark, brick exterior of the Thompsons' home and a bloody handprint on the garage behind the Eriksons' home next door, "where Mrs. Carol Thompson first went in her frantic search for help."

The *Star* provided a front-page montage that included a wide shot of the Thompsons' block, with a broken arrow describing Carol's erratic path to the Nelsons'. T. Eugene Thompson was the subject of the second photo—a short, boyish, grim-faced man in a military-style brush cut and dark-rimmed glasses, neatly dressed in a white shirt, dark suit, and dark tie—surrounded by friends, reporters, and detectives at Ancker Hospital. A third photo revealed a white-gowned physician giving Mrs. Thompson a "heart massage" en route to the hospital's operating room. The victim's face and body were obscured by towels and sheets, but her bare right arm was plainly visible, as was enough blood to suggest the seriousness of her trauma.

9.

Donald John Giese was only one of several dozen reporters marshaled to cover the Carol Thompson homicide that day by the *Dispatch*; its morning sibling, the *Pioneer Press*; both the *Minneapolis Star* and morning *Tribune*; the local bureaus of the Associated Press and United Press International; Twin Cities radio and television stations, including the local affiliates of the three major networks; and news organizations across the state.

But it was Giese, recalling the situation several years later, who best summed up the community's response to the day's extraordinary events:

Northwestern Bell Telephone Company lines carried extra-heavy loads that Wednesday afternoon. Husbands called their wives and instructed them to keep doors and windows locked and not to answer the door until they got home from work. Wives called their husbands at their offices and told them to come home early. Hardware stores did a brisk business in chain locks that afternoon and sporting goods stores had an unusual run on shotgun shells and rifle and pistol cartridges.... Gas and electric meter readers had to pass up many homes where their knocks went unanswered. Mailmen carrying special delivery letters or packages, door-to-door salesmen and fund solicitors knocked on doors and rang doorbells in vain. Women, home alone, pushed aside curtains, looked through windows, shook their heads, and waved all but close friends away....

All that day and late that night a steady stream of cars drove slowly by 1720 Hillcrest Avenue, stopping briefly in the street in front of the Thompson home, and then moving on again when the driver in the car immediately behind honked his horn.

All the Angels

1.

At about eight o'clock on Thursday morning, February 28, 1963, Einar Nelson, an employee of the Minneapolis Park Board, was walking his spaniel in Minnehaha Park before going to work. A few feet off a foot path near the park's ski slide he came across a girl's body lying face down in the snow. The girl—who would quickly be identified as a fifteen-year-old Catholic high school sophomore named Mary Louise Bell—had been stabbed forty-five times and beaten nearly beyond recognition.

The story of Mary Bell's murder was front-page news in Twin Cities papers and led the day's local radio and television news-casts. Photos of the girl living and dead—bright-eyed and smiling in a mortarboard and gown at her junior high graduation less than a year earlier, then shapeless and anonymous beneath a plaid blanket in the snowy park—graphically displayed the before-and-after rupture caused by violent crime.

For many Twin Citians, the case suggested an unsettling proximity to violent death. If you lived on the South Side of Minneapolis, in the near-south suburbs, or on the other side of the Ford Bridge spanning the Mississippi—that is, in the Highland Park or Macalester-Groveland neighborhood of St. Paul—Minnehaha Park was your common backyard. Minnehaha Park was to south-metro Twin Citians what Central Park was to New Yorkers, though, unlike Central Park or at least Twin Citians' distant perception of it, Minnehaha Park was still a safe place to picnic, hike, and find some sylvan privacy with a friend or lover. No one, except perhaps a few of the older veterans of the Minneapolis Police Department, could remember the last homicide reported anywhere within its almost two hundred wooded, hilly acres. The Bells, moreover, were a large, white, working-class family of the size and composition present in every South Side neighborhood. Pretty, gregarious Mary Bell herself was the kind of teenaged girl whom everybody knew—if not directly, then at a remove of only one or two degrees, as, say, the best friend of the girl you sat next to in French class.

Gruesome and close to home as it was, though, Mary Bell's murder lacked mystery almost from the start, so the fear it sparked—of a homicidal maniac who preyed on teenaged girls—was short-lived, almost nonexistent. The killer, a nineteen-year-old car thief on parole from the state reformatory at St. Cloud, was in custody by nightfall of the day Mary's body was discovered. By the end of the following day, Ronald Steeves had abandoned a series of improbable alibis and confessed to the crime. And Steeves's rationale turned out to be as mindless and banal as it was brutal and sad. Against the wishes of the girls' parents, he had been dating Mary's older sister. Furious that Mary had told her parents about the relationship, he had abducted her from a late-night baby-sitting job and driven her to the nearby park, where he dragged her down a footpath in the dark and stabbed her repeatedly with a pocketknife. When "she wouldn't die," he told investigators, he beat her with a tire iron that he had brought from his car. Five days later, Steeves was indicted on charges of first-degree murder. He pleaded guilty and was sentenced to life in prison.

In 1963, the Twin Cities was a prosperous, growing, yet still decidedly mid-sized, "clean," and homogeneous seven-county metropolitan area of a million-and-a-half people. By the end of the year, probably fewer than thirty metro residents would be murder victims. Most of those would be adult males who died at the hands of other adult males, more often than not during the commission of another crime or in the heat of jealousy or passion, frequently fueled by alcohol. A disproportionate number of victims and murderers would be African American or American Indian, and most would be poor or indigent. When a man murdered a woman—almost always the dynamic when the killer and victim were of the opposite sex—they almost always knew each other, if only for an evening. Most female victims were the killer's wife or girlfriend, current or former.

Mary Bell's murder was memorable because both the victim and her killer were only in their teens and because the act itself was so vicious. It shook local sensibilities, gave lovely Minnehaha Park a brief notoriety, and perhaps brought families with teenaged boys and girls a little closer together, at least for a while. But, as a subject of public wonder, dread, and speculation, the case was quickly overwhelmed by the shock waves that followed Carol Thompson's murder, only six days after Mary Bell's.

2.

What made the Thompson case stand out at the beginning was, of course, the station and character of the victim, juxtaposed against the baffling, almost surreal circumstances of her murder and the mystery of her killer's identity. Why her? Why here? Initially, almost anything seemed possible. Reporter Kathryn Boardman, writing in the *Pioneer Press* the next day, expressed the range of possibilities: Carol Thompson "apparently died through some frightful quirk of fate that may involve chance, mistaken identity, revenge, or madness on the part of [her] killer."

The early hypothesis that one of T. Eugene Thompson's clients or courtroom adversaries had exacted vengeance on his wife offered reason to believe that Carol had been a specific target. George Barkley's comments, published by the *Star* a few hours after the assault, describing Mrs. Thompson opening her front door to a man who hit her over the head, then beat and stabbed her, reinforced the likelihood of a premeditated attack that would be perversely reassuring to the general public spooked by the idea of a random slaying.

On the other hand, the disarray in the Thompsons' bedroom, described in the next morning's papers, suggested a more plausible—and frightening—scenario: A stranger had entered the Thompson home intending to burglarize it, had been surprised by Mrs. Thompson, and had murdered her in order to finish the job and escape. Rare as such a crime would have been in the Twin Cities at the time, it could have happened to anyone, in any neighborhood—not only to the wife of a "prominent attorney" in comfortable Highland Park—and that made it a terrifying possibility for all.

In any case, if safe, solid Hillcrest Avenue was an unlikely site for a home invasion and murder, Carol Swoboda Thompson was an implausible casualty. Several acquaintances, struggling to make sense of the crime in its immediate aftermath, told reporters that

Carol Thompson was literally the last person in the world they could imagine meeting such a fate. Her "official" photograph—a black-and-white studio portrait cropped tight around her head and shoulders and displayed so often by Twin Cities newspapers and television stations during the following several months that it became eerily iconic—showed a pretty, dark-haired, round-faced woman wearing pearl earrings, the tortoiseshell cat's-eye glasses fashionable at the time, and a toothy, guileless smile. Given her age, hairstyle, and demeanor, she could have been the slightly younger sister of another wholesome face born and bred in the Twin Cities: General Mills' all-American homemaker, Betty Crocker. If you were a kid of, say, fifteen or under, Carol Thompson could have been your mom.

Newspaper and broadcast reports described Mrs. Thompson as the paradigm of the early sixties wife and mother. Those few of her many friends who were not too shaken by her death to comment publicly agreed that she was intelligent, principled, caring, talented, cheerful, fun-loving, and popular. "She was very much an extrovert, much known and much loved by everyone," the Thompsons' pastor, the Reverend William Paden, told a *Pioneer Press* reporter on March 6. According to Paden and other friends at nearby Edgcumbe Presbyterian Church, where the Thompsons were charter members, Mrs. Thompson taught a kindergarten Sunday school class, supervised the church's floral decoration, and was past president of its women's association. "She was a terrific gal and my girl Friday," said Mrs. Ralph Kuehn, who chaired the neighborhood Girl Scout organization. "Her [Brownie] troop loved her."

Other friends described Carol as "interested in everything," the *Pioneer Press* reported on March 7, in a recitation of testimonials to the dead woman by baffled and grief-stricken acquaintances.

"She would sit down with [her] children when they came home

from school and have a milk shake and talk things over with them," one friend told the paper.

"She was always trying to gain more knowledge," said another. "Although she was an excellent knitter, she took lessons to learn to do it better. She also liked to read."

"Mrs. Thompson was active in the Lawyers' Wives organization and she and her husband belonged to a couples' bridge club," the paper said. "She was considered an excellent bridge player."

"She was an inspiration," said a friend.

The basic data were reported and repeated in the papers. But a more comprehensive biography and family history—the latter particularly important in St. Paul, a conservative and status-conscious community where lineage and marriage were keenly noted—derived from public records and less intimate sources emerged over the next several days. This less subjective but often exaggerated information was the topic of countless conversations in barbershops, beauty parlors, club rooms, restaurants, taverns, and breakfast nooks throughout the Twin Cities.

Carol's father, Otto Swoboda, was a successful plumbing and heating contractor well known in St. Paul business circles. The son of Czech immigrants, he had been raised in Badger, a tiny community in northwestern Minnesota. Largely self-taught and industrious, he had come to the Twin Cities as a young man and learned shorthand and other clerical skills in night school. He took a job keeping the books for the D. W. Hickey Company on University Avenue and eventually bought the firm from its founder. Swoboda now counted among his customers the 3M Company and several other major corporations. Quietly confident and self-contained, he was widely respected for both his business acumen and personal probity. Carol's mother, Antonia, or "Toni" to family and friends, was a diminutive, intelligent, and forceful woman with firm opinions—a no-nonsense former schoolteacher with Bohemian roots from Yankton, South Dakota. (A "strong, courageous, and serene woman," a reporter observed, shortly after her daughter's murder.) The Swobodas were not old money in a town that revered it, but they were, by the early 1960s, unostentatiously well-to-do and respectable.

Carol Ann was born on October 11, 1928, in St. Paul. By all accounts, she was a bright, well-behaved child who loved music and gave her strict but doting parents little cause for worry. Despite her father's financial success and her status as an only child, Carol was not coddled. Her parents expected her to make something of herself and to do so on the strength of her brains, talent, and resourcefulness.

Though her father could have afforded to send her to nearby Summit School, a private academy for wealthy girls, Carol attended public schools in Highland Park, where her parents had settled in 1934. She graduated from James Monroe High School in 1946, twenty-third out of her class of 230, and was later described as "an excellent student of well above average intelligence." After high school, she went on to Macalester College, a small, highly regarded, and relatively expensive liberal arts institution situated on a leafy campus off Grand Avenue. There she majored in English, studied Russian and library science, and fell in love with a self-assured young Navy veteran known to friends as Cotton Thompson.

Carol's parents were probably not enthusiastic about her quitting college during her sophomore year to get married, but their affection for Thompson—a smart and engaging former small-town boy determined to make something of himself in the big city, much as Otto had done—was obvious and apparently unreserved. Otto proudly gave his daughter away as Toni looked on approvingly when Carol and Cotton were married in a small, dignified ceremony at St. Paul's Unity Church, on March 27, 1948, not quite a year after the couple met. The Swobodas' fondness for

Thompson only grew after the marriage, the differences in the newlyweds' backgrounds proving, if they had ever been a concern, to be of no account.

While Cotton continued his studies, he and Carol worked odd jobs on and off campus; they also received financial help from both Carol's parents and Cotton's father, Tilmer, who farmed and operated a chicken hatchery in Elmore, Minnesota. The couple's first home was a one-room efficiency apartment in a converted storefront on St. Clair Avenue, close to the Macalester campus. Later, they moved into temporary housing in a Quonset-hut complex known as Macalester Village—"Macville" for short. In the fall of 1948, Carol was pregnant with their first child, who was born on June 20, 1949, and named Jeffrey Douglas.

Whatever dreams she might have had for herself, Carol was now, according to family and friends, content to be a wife and mother. It was the role she performed, seemingly to perfection, until the day she died.

3.

The police, meanwhile, were urgently developing their own biography of Carol Thompson. It would be a life story based on dozens of confidential and presumably candid interviews with relatives, friends, and neighbors.

Some of the details that acquaintances told investigators could have been viewed as ambiguous, questionable, and no one's business but that of those involved. Even so, in the beginning, the detectives' narrative, for the most part, ran parallel to, not divergent from, the more general data collected, assembled, and presented by the media for public consumption.

Investigators were interested, of course, in reports of an admirer—the window salesman who was first mentioned by T. Eugene Thompson on March 6. A tall, handsome redhead in his early thirties, Kenneth Moran* told police that he had known the Thompsons for almost a year, since selling them combination windows and doors for the house. He said he had occasionally visited the Thompson home as both a salesman and a friend, accompanied Carol to nearby art museums, and driven her and the children to the "summer home" the Thompsons shared with Carol's parents on Forest Lake, north of the city. Moran said, however, that he had not seen Carol since the previous November and knew nothing about her murder. He had an alibi for the time of the attack (his boss confirmed that Moran had been at a sales meeting that morning) and later passed a polygraph examination. Nonetheless, his name—or, more often, his nickname, "Big Red"— came up in many of the early conversations between the police and Carol's friends.

Typical was the conversation between Grant Willinger and Mrs. Harold Erikson, the Thompsons' next-door neighbor, five days after Carol's murder. Merlyn Erikson told the detective that she had "never heard of either Mr. or Mrs. Thompson having any boy or girl friends or any mention of any contemplated divorce." She did, however, know of the window salesman, who did indeed have "an infatuation" with Carol. "This feeling was not returned per Carol, who told Mrs. Erickson [sic] about it," Willinger reported. "Carol said that she did not dislike [the salesman] and was attracted to him, but loved only her husband and children." Carol and the salesman never dated, Mrs. Erikson said, but on at least one occasion he took "his family" to visit Carol and the Thompson children at Forest Lake. On another occasion, Mrs. Erikson told Willinger, Mr. Thompson came home in the middle of the af-

* Actual names have been used throughout this account except where noted by an asterisk. The author has changed the names of four individuals whose association with the events described here was not criminal yet could prove embarrassing to innocent persons.

ternoon and found the man in the backyard, chatting with Carol. Mr. Thompson became angry and told him to stay away, which "perturbed" Carol, Mrs. Erikson said. But, afterward, Mr. Thompson was "more attentive" to Carol and the kids, "for which Carol was thankful."

Clara Neptune, who lived two houses east of the Thompsons, concurred with Mrs. Erikson's account, and told Willinger that she believed Carol was "incapable of having an affair."

Yvonne Bengel, one door to the west, said that Carol had told *her*, when she asked about Kenneth Moran's visits the previous summer, "It's strictly a platonic friendship. We share the same interests."

Later the same day, Willinger talked to another friend of Carol's, Mrs. Robert Erickson. The Thompsons and the Ericksons had been close for several years and spent a great deal of time together both in the city and at Forest Lake. Of Carol's relationship with Moran, Marian Erickson said, according to Willinger, "Carol was capable of handling the situation without getting too involved, [although] she was attracted to him." If, in the meantime, there had been problems between Carol and Cotton, Carol would have confided in her. Mrs. Erickson was certain that, in any case, Carol "loved her family above all else."

Other friends told detectives similar stories and offered similar conclusions.

Additional intelligence developed by the police during those early interviews included the following bits and pieces:

Carol had been a shy child and young adult. She had overcome her shyness by getting involved in church groups, scout troops, a bridge club, and other social organizations, "to the point where she was quite self-possessed."

Carol was an excellent seamstress who took a quiet pride in making her daughters' coats and dresses. Though her husband liked to dress expensively, Carol was content with the dresses she made for herself. While Cotton was ambitious and hard-driving, "Carol was satisfied with her home, club meetings, etc."

Even as an up-and-coming attorney's wife, Carol retained her "conservative nature." She employed a cleaning lady, but had her come only once a month. She had her hair done at Power's department store on Ford Parkway instead of at a downtown salon. While Cotton drove a new (or nearly new) Oldsmobile station wagon, Carol was happy to zip around town in a three-year-old Volkswagen Beetle. Her private pleasures included reading novels and listening to popular music.

Carol liked to travel. She often accompanied her husband on trips he took as an officer or committeeman of state and national bar associations. A month before Carol's death, the couple enjoyed a combined business and pleasure trip to New Orleans. In the past few years, the couple had traveled to Florida, Washington, D.C., Chicago, Las Vegas, and San Francisco, occasionally with the children, but more often as a couple mixing business meetings with shopping and nightlife. On more than one occasion, Carol told her friends that she and Cotton had discussed the possibility of living abroad—in Mexico or Peru, for instance—where they would learn the culture not as tourists but as residents, students, or volunteers in the Peace Corps, the federal government's new international assistance program.

Carol had also expressed interest, as her children grew older, in returning to school, earning a bachelor's degree in library science, and going to work, at least part-time, at the Highland Park public library. She had also told friends that she would like to resume the Russian-language studies she had begun at Macalester and some day travel to the Soviet Union.

In the several weeks before her murder, she was excited about the redecoration of her home. In January and February, the living- and dining-room walls were painted robin's egg blue—her favorite color—and expensive new carpeting had been installed on the main floor.

Carol was concerned about her propensity to gain weight and had recently begun a modest diet under her doctor's supervision. (The county's autopsy report recorded her weight at one hundred forty pounds, which would have been somewhat excessive for her five-foot, four-inch frame. She was otherwise, according to the pathologist's report, in excellent health.)

Carol did not smoke. She had at one time, but then only after dinner. She had quit several years earlier.

Carol had never been much of a drinker, preferring, when the couple went out, to nurse a single cocktail over the course of an evening. At home, she drank sparingly, and usually only when entertaining. "She was such a lively person anyway that she did not need alcohol to pep her up," her friend Marian Erickson said.

Carol was extremely nearsighted. She wore her glasses virtually every waking moment, taking them off only when she bathed or swam. She would never have answered the door without her glasses, friends said. For that matter, "Carol would not open the door to a stranger, especially the way she was dressed"—that is, wearing only a bathrobe, which was all she had on when she appeared at the Nelsons' front door on the morning of March 6.

"Carol was the type of person who would fight like a wildcat if attacked and was quite strong."

4.

Given Carol Thompson's many friends and involvements, it was reasonable to believe that several acquaintances, immediately following her death, would be able to help investigators recreate her last days.

Marian Erickson told Detective Buechner that on Saturday evening, March 2, Carol and Cotton had dined out with two other couples, including old Macalester friends who were visiting over the weekend. The next day the Thompsons attended Sunday morning services at Edgcumbe Presbyterian, a few blocks from their home. Carol taught Sunday school, the girls went to their Sunday school classes, and Cotton and Jeff heard the Reverend Paden preach his Sunday sermon. Afterward, the family remained at church for coffee hour, then stopped by the Ericksons' for more coffee and conversation. "Sunday was family day for the Thompsons," Buechner wrote, apparently quoting Mrs. Erickson. That Sunday, the Thompsons were debating whether to spend the afternoon at the Minneapolis Institute of Arts, which was Carol's preference, or to see the new Disney movie, *Son of Flubber,* which Cotton and the children wanted to do. The following day, Carol told Mrs. Erickson that "*Son of Flubber* won."

On Monday, March 4, Carol again dropped in at the Ericksons'. The Ericksons had just purchased a hi-fi set, and Carol brought over a half-dozen albums for Marian to hear. Carol was very fond of music, Mrs. Erickson told Buechner. "She made me promise to listen to her records. In fact, she said she would quiz me about them later." Mrs. Erickson rattled off the names of the albums and their performers: *The Sound of Music,* with Mary Martin; *Film Encores,* by Mantovani; *Reverie* and *Songs of the World,* by the Norman Luboff Choir; *Belafonte Sings of the Caribbean.* Carol also brought along a couple of books she thought Marian would enjoy: *Touring with Towser,* "in case we ever wanted to take our dog with us on a trip," Marian explained, and *Ring of Bright Water,* an unlikely best-seller about a pair of otters, by Gavin Maxwell. When she left, Carol borrowed two of her friend's records—albums by the Kingston Trio and the Brothers Four—to play at home. "She had to leave because she was picking Amy up at a friend's house at five," Mrs. Erickson said.

Yet another friend, Virginia Koutsky, who with her husband,

Carl, was part of a dinner group with the Thompsons and the Ericksons, told Detective Donald Blakely that she had twice spoken to Carol by phone on Tuesday, March 5. Carol called at about seven, but Mrs. Koutsky had been too busy to chat, so she called Carol back a couple of hours later. The women talked about the knitting class they were planning to attend Wednesday evening at Como Junior High School, Blakely reported. "Carol told [Mrs. Koutsky] she'd had a hectic day, but was in good spirits as usual." Blakely continued: "Carol had told her some time ago she wished Gene would spend more time with the family and enjoy the kids like other husbands and fathers. More recently, Carol indicated she had made an adjustment to him and realized he was too busy to give them any more time. Carol never indicated she suspected Gene of chasing any women, nor did she ever say they were having any marital problems. Nothing was ever mentioned about divorce."

If Virginia Koutsky was correct about a knitting class on Wednesday, it would have had to be later that night, because Mrs. Owen Olson, another Edgcumbe Presbyterian member, told Detective Willinger that she and Carol were supervising a supper of the church's Youth Fellowship Club on Wednesday evening. In fact, Mrs. Olson said, she called the Thompson home at exactly 8:35 the morning of the sixth regarding the arrangements.

She told the detective that she had waited until after eight-thirty so Carol would have time to see her family off to work and school before having to review the supper details. She said she had let the phone ring at least six times, but there had been no response.

5.

No less interesting to the public, the media, and the police—virtually from the moment Carol Thompson's homicide was reported—

was her husband. Indeed, within days of the murder, Tilmer Eugene Thompson's life would become as much an open book as his wife's.

His official biography was at once unremarkable in its broad outline and interesting in its detail. Thompson was born in Blue Earth, Minnesota, on August 7, 1927, and brought up in nearby Elmore, population less than a thousand, on the Iowa border three hours south of the Twin Cities. Tilmer Eugene was the fifth of seven children—four boys and three girls—two of whom died young in traffic accidents. Young Cotton, so called because of his white-blond shock of hair, was bookish and ambitious. He was an avid reader and loved to debate. He attended the Elmore public schools, where he and another bright, ambitious boy, Walter "Fritz" Mondale, played football, were elected class officers, and supposedly shared grand plans for the future. According to Thompson family lore, Fritz and Cotton decided they would study law and enter public life. If they had their way and enjoyed a little luck, Mondale would one day be elected president of the United States and Thompson would be appointed chief justice of the United States Supreme Court.*

During his senior year at Elmore High, Cotton abruptly dropped out of school and enlisted in the Navy, lying about his age (he was seventeen) to be allowed in. He was apparently eager to follow in the tracks of older brother Donald. It was early 1945, near the end of World War II. Cotton would serve for almost eighteen months, part of that time aboard a minesweeper in the South Pacific, before being honorably discharged in July 1946.

Returning to Minnesota, he enrolled at Macalester College, where his tuition was covered by the newly enacted G.I. Bill. He

* Walter Mondale—who would, in fact, be elected U.S. senator and vice president and eventually run for president—was Minnesota's attorney general in 1963. He also attended Macalester during the late 1940s.

majored in economics, minored in political science and Spanish, and began dating a comely, dark-haired coed named Carol Swoboda in early 1947. He and Carol were married less than a year later.

As Thompson later told the story, the day after his graduation in January 1950 he went to work for the Household Finance Corporation in Minneapolis, investigating and evaluating applicants for home loans and earning $180 a month. When he quit that job about fifteen months later to enroll in evening classes at the St. Paul College of Law, his monthly income had jumped to $380, a reflection, it seemed, of his drive and resourcefulness. He earned his law school tuition working days for the City and County Employees Credit Union in St. Paul. He and Carol were fortunate, in addition, to have generous parents. The couple often received gifts, including cash, from the Swobodas and Tilmer Thompson. (His mother, Josephine Thompson, had died in 1950.) And in 1953, when Cotton and Carol, after several years of renting apartments, bought a house on Rome Avenue in Highland Park, Otto Swoboda lent them the money. Five years later, Swoboda helped cover the mortgage on their second, larger house, at 1720 Hillcrest, a few blocks from the first.

Cotton, by his own admission, had a healthy appreciation of money, and he was eager to work for it. Besides his job with the credit union, he acquired an insurance agent's license from the state and sold casualty insurance on the side. He also worked part-time for his father-in-law's plumbing and heating company—"help[ing] around the office, do[ing] whatever I could," he explained years later.

Like most husbands of his time, he did not think his wife should work outside the home. How could she? The couple had three children by their seventh wedding anniversary, with Patricia and Margaret joining Jeff in 1951 and 1953. At any rate, upon his graduation from law school in June 1955, his passing of the state bar examination a month later, and his immediate hiring by the St. Paul firm of Hoffman, Donahue, and Graff, Cotton Thompson was on his way to what would surely be a lucrative career. His wife, he had determined, would never have to work.

Thompson immersed himself in a busy practice that included, he said later, divorce, personal injury, and a handful of criminal cases. He was also hired as the village attorney of suburban North St. Paul and became active in state and national bar associations. He even managed to teach a few classes at his alma mater, by then renamed the William Mitchell College of Law.

By the time he was thirty, Cotton Thompson was living an estimable and envied life that in many ways exemplified that of the ascendant American family man in the bountiful years that followed World War II. A background report prepared for an insurance company in 1962 said his "potential appear[ed] to be unlimited."

6.

In the first few days following his wife's murder, the Twin Cities media repeated the basic biographical data. Reporters described T. Eugene Thompson as a "prominent" St. Paul attorney, without either elaborating on or offering much proof of his prominence in the city's legal community. The newspapers projected the image of a bereft husband and partnerless father who was cooperating with the police as best he could. They excused his polite but firm refusal to speak at any length to the reporters deployed on Hillcrest Avenue, at his Minnesota Building office, and in the corridor outside the homicide division of the Public Safety Building, where he was filmed and photographed coming and going, straight-backed, square-jawed, and stone-faced, a rather small man (reportedly five feet, seven inches tall) invariably dressed to the nines in a well-tailored suit and snap-brim fedora. Don Giese described Thompson's response as "studied indifference—he neither attempts to get attention nor, having gotten it, does he make any attempt to hide."

Out of the media glare, George Barkley's detectives were gathering their own intelligence about Thompson. Their sources, at the outset, were the same relatives, friends, and neighbors who were providing the details and insights about Carol. And like the private wife and mother who emerged interview by interview—as a photographic image emerges from its negative—the private husband and father at first diverged only slightly from the public persona.

Friends told the detectives, for instance, that Thompson was smart and ambitious, was money- and status-conscious, and liked to dress expensively. Unlike some of the husbands in the Thompsons' circle, Cotton did not care to hunt and fish—"Gene was more the indoor type who likes plays," said a friend—though he did enjoy water sports during outings at Forest Lake. He was active in his church, at various times an elder and a member of the choir. He kept busy and worked hard. He was away from the house a great deal, presumably on business or taking part in professional committee activities.

One friend described Thompson as a "devoted student of the law." The friend said Cotton loved to teach when he had the time and talked about going back to school, increasing his knowledge and credentials, and maybe, with his wife, someday studying and teaching abroad. Education at all levels was important to him. A year earlier, Cotton had removed Jeff from public school and enrolled him in the more demanding St. Paul Academy. Cotton had been monitoring Jeff's academic progress closely that first year at s.p.a., and he was said to be pleased with the results.

Cotton was on good terms with Carol's parents and his siblings, just as Carol had enjoyed friendly relations with his sisters and brother. But his mother was dead, and he had little to do with his father, from whom he had been estranged for some time (though, apparently, not so estranged that he would not accept the occasional monetary gift from the older man). Friends understood that Cotton's father had deserted the family and moved in with another woman when Cotton was a boy and that Cotton had never forgiven him. A few years before her death, Carol had persuaded Cotton to visit his father when the latter was hospitalized in Rochester, but no one seemed to think there was ever a rapprochement.

In any event, Cotton seemed to have found paternal surrogates in both Otto Swoboda, his father-in-law, part-time employer, and "banker," and Jerome Hoffman, who brought the green attorney into his firm and advised him on matters ranging from the practice of law to the way a successful lawyer should dress. The Thompsons' good friends, Douglas and Marjorie Young, happened to be with Cotton the day, in 1958, that Hoffman died, and Cotton, said Mrs. Young, had been "very broken up about it."

At first glance, there seemed to be little that set Thompson apart from his hardworking, family oriented, upwardly mobile friends and neighbors. His preoccupation with money was hardly unusual among his social set. Who didn't want to earn a robust income and provide well for his family? He was part of a generation of young men who had been raised during the Great Depression and had put their futures on hold while they fought in a world war. They had done their duty and paid their dues, and now they were going to make the most of what prosperous postwar America had to offer them.

If Cotton cared a bit more than his friends about money and had more exotic tastes and plans—well, that was just Cotton. He liked to talk, to show off—even boasting of special powers, such as an ability to see into the future that he had claimed since he was a kid. There was, moreover, an undeniable flair, a charisma, about him. He was lively, colorful, and fun to be around. He was a *char-*

acter. Friends said that even if it was difficult to *like* him the way you liked—no, *loved*—Carol, there was no denying his intelligence and drive. He was going to make something of himself. Probably sooner than later.

But, as close acquaintances spoke about the Thompsons, they revealed other, less flattering—or at least less explicable—information about the new widower.

With the kind of indulgent language that accompanies descriptions of especially self-centered children and eccentrics, friends noted that Cotton's penchant for fashionable clothes sometimes ran to foppish extravagance. He was sometimes known, for instance, to swagger around downtown, in some of the city's better-known club rooms and watering holes, sporting a derby and brandishing a cane with a silver handle and tip. He carried thick rolls of cash in his pockets and stashed sizable amounts of money around the house. He sometimes carried a gun in his briefcase, and he boasted of being an honorary St. Paul police officer. He liked to play the big shot, to be the center of attention. Some friends also described him as self-absorbed and narcissistic. He could be cold and aloof, they said.

Sooner or later, when pressed by investigators, most everyone in the Thompsons' circle would get around to Cotton's not-so-subtle interest in other women—which, if the couple's friends could be believed, seemed to bother no one, not even Carol.

"Gene was a constant flirt," Detective Willinger reported after an extensive conversation with Marj Young. "[W]hile he didn't make any overt act, both Mrs. Young and Mrs. Koutsky made it a point not to be alone with him for fear he would [make an advance] and spoil a friendship." After his discussion with Virginia Koutsky, Detective Blakely wrote: "Gene did like women and often put his hand on [Mrs. Koutsky's] knee, but he did it to all the girls and no one took him seriously. Carol said he was like a dog chasing a car and wouldn't know what to do if he caught it." Carl

Koutsky told Blakely that "the girls regarded Gene as harmless" and "[Koutsky] had no reason to believe otherwise."

Neither Carol nor Cotton, according to their closest friends, ever spoke of discord between them. For all his flirtatiousness, no one seemed to believe that Cotton was capable of an extramarital affair, much less of leaving Carol for another woman.

"Gene would not be easy to live with," Willinger quoted Marj Young as saying, but she had never heard any talk about divorce. As a matter of fact, the couple had within the previous few weeks spent a sizable amount of money redecorating their home, which, in hindsight, struck some friends as proof that the Thompsons' marriage was solid. "[Carol] commented that Cotton couldn't buy just a chair, but had to do the whole bit," Willinger reported after talking to Mrs. Young. The last time she saw Carol alive, on February 27, Willinger quoted her as saying, "Carol and Cotton and I chatted ... about how nice everything looked, and discussed the pros and cons of the various accessories the decorator left on approval." Apparently, the only unfortunate aspect of the redecoration was the need for Cotton to get rid of the family's three-year-old dachshund. The Thompsons were afraid that Schatzie, who had never been properly house-trained, would ruin the new carpeting.

On Tuesday evening, March 5, Cotton and Doug Young talked on the telephone. Though it was already after nine, Cotton invited his friend to come over, presumably to enjoy a nightcap. But Young declined, because, he told Cotton, Marj's folks were visiting from out of town.

According to police reports, none of the familiar sources believed that Thompson had anything to do with his wife's murder. Cotton was devastated by Carol's death, friends said. The tears, anguish, and concern for his children were genuine and profound. The night of the murder, Doug Young would recall later, Thompson had wailed, "Carol, what have I done to you?" But, said

Young, the small group of family members and friends that surrounded Thompson that evening attributed the outburst to a combination of grief, liquor, and his natural inclination toward self-dramatization. "We were afraid that he might somehow harm himself," Young told Don Giese.

If friends gave any credence to his claims of clairvoyance, they would have had to believe that Cotton was unnerved by intimations of Carol's death for some time before it happened. Cotton told Marj Young (as she later told the police) that for several weeks prior to the murder he had "nightmares" involving his wife. According to Giese, Carol had told her mother that in late February and the first couple days of March she had had to rouse Cotton from "bad dreams about violent death." "Carol said Gene was going through some kind of torture in his sleep," Mrs. Swoboda told the reporter, "and when he screamed she woke him up and he told her he had dreamed something terrible had happened."

Antonia Swoboda, who was known to believe in "spiritual" phenomena herself, added, said Giese: "Shortly before Carol's death Gene told me he didn't know what he would do if anything ever happened to her. Then after the murder he was stunned over the freakish, terrible thing that suddenly happened."

7.

Almost simultaneously with the compilation of those acquaintance reports, Barkley's investigators were hearing about T. Eugene Thompson from several less sympathetic sources, probably not entirely to the detectives' surprise.

Of course, Thompson had an unimpeachable alibi for the morning of March 6. According to his secretary, Kathleen Zajacz, his officemate, Donald Kelly, and other Minnesota Building regulars, he was at work downtown from about eight-thirty until Sidney Nelson called him at the office a few minutes after nine. Still, when a woman is murdered, detectives usually look first at her husband or boyfriend. And unsolicited reports reaching police headquarters almost immediately after word of the murder hit the Twin Cities' streets gave the detectives cause to be suspicious.

Thompson's acquaintances in the local underworld were—as Thompson himself suggested when he offered to review his client list after the murder—worth a look. The late Jerry Hoffman, Thompson's mentor, had had a reputation in some quarters as being a "lawyer to the Mob," but what *that* had to do with the Thompsons was at best unclear. Of greater interest was the information, acquired from an unnamed informant by Detective Williams the day after the murder, that three major insurance companies—Travelers, Continental Casualty, and Lloyds of London—had written, in the previous thirteen months, accidental-death policies on the life of Carol Thompson totaling $900,000. The beneficiary, according to Williams' source, was T. Eugene Thompson, who had purchased the last of the several policies less than two months before the murder. Ramsey County's chief prosecutor, William Randall, learned of the Thompsons' outsized insurance policies from a neighbor, at about the same time. Within the next couple of days, Continental Casualty's chief investigator had flown to St. Paul from the company's home office in Chicago and helped the detectives revise their initial information. Thompson in fact owned policies on his wife's life from at least eight separate insurers, and the value of those policies upon Carol's death, either accidental or of "any type," totaled $1.061 *million*. That was, by everybody's reckoning, an extraordinary amount to carry on even an extraordinary housewife in 1963, when the average American earned less than $10,000 a year and the average sales price of a home in the Twin Cities was under $20,000. Thompson himself was insured to the amount of $400,000, which was no insignificant sum, yet seemed paltry compared with the amount written on his wife, especially inasmuch as he was the family's breadwinner.

Other reports, mostly from unnamed sources, suggested that Thompson was more than the harmless flirt described by friends and neighbors. Typical of that line of information was the intelligence given to a St. Paul police officer named Dennis Klinge by an "anonymous friend," who said that a switchboard operator at a North St. Paul construction company "knows a girl who is supposed to have lived in an apartment paid for by Mr. Thompson." "How long ago, I don't know," the source said. "She, this girl, finally married someone else, apparently after realizing Mr. Thompson wasn't going to get a divorce."

On March 8, Detective Bodin reported this conversation from "an anonymous woman caller": "I can tell you why that Thompson woman was killed. Her husband was running around with another woman. If you get hold of Dick Sharp of Minneapolis, he knows the two men who were hired to do the job."

An "anonymous male caller" told Detective McLaughlin that a Vicky Miller, "who is, or was, married" to one Michael Miller and had been a secretary to T. Eugene Thompson, "has gone on trips with Thompson to Chicago."* The informant told McLaughlin that Thompson had "offered to finance the cost incurred in the divorce proceedings" between the Millers. "It is further alleged by this informant that a note, written by Michael Miller to Carol Thompson, and containing information relative to Thompson's going out with other women, was destroyed by Thompson" or by a private investigator Thompson had employed.

Information from other sources also focused investigators' attention on Victoria—"Vicky"—Miller. One report reached Bodin through a functionary at the city's housing authority, who said he

---

* These are not their real names.

had been told almost two years earlier about a divorcée named Victoria living in one of the authority's subsidized duplexes, who had been in a "thick relationship" with Thompson. The latter, said Bodin's source, "made frequent trips to visit [the woman], and took her on at least one out-of-town trip."

In response to Barkley's public plea for information immediately following the murder and then to the offer of a $1,000 reward posted by KSTP Radio and Television a few days later, dozens of letters were delivered to both the Public Safety Building and KSTP studios. Most reflected the fear and confusion that gripped the Twin Cities in the wake of the slaying, pointing to "strange" neighbors and "unkempt" strangers whom the letter-writers had observed around town. Some suggested that the case was beyond the capabilities of the St. Paul police, and one proposed the hiring of Dutch psychic Peter Hurkos, who had been involved in several well-publicized murder and missing-person investigations around the world.

Several letters, however, made at least a veiled reference to T. Eugene Thompson's alleged philandering, and some provided enough specifics to sound credible. "Check Mr. Thompson more carefully," read one. "Ask him when he was in Chicago last and if there was another woman there." Some of the letters, most of them unsigned, referred to the same woman. One anonymous author wrote: "Eugene Thompson shacked up with and supported Vicky Miller whose first husband was Robert Larson* and she has remarried and both husbands are furious with Eugene. Check all the angels [sic]."

Lest anyone forget that St. Paul was still, in many respects, a small town where much that had to do with other people's business was carefully observed and summarily evaluated, there were

* Not his real name.

messages like this one, too: "Mrs. Thompson was buried on Saturday. On Saturday evening Mr. Thompson was enjoying the hospitality of The Lexington," a popular restaurant and bar on Grand Avenue. "He did not have the appearance of a heart-broken, bereaved husband." In truth, Doug Young said years later, the "attractive blonde" that Thompson was seen with that night at the Lex was one of T. Eugene's sisters.

On Tuesday, March 12, six days after Carol's murder, detectives picked up Victoria and Michael Miller at their apartment in St. Paul's blue-collar Frogtown neighborhood, where they lived with Vicky's three small children, and brought them downtown for an interview. According to Detective Blakely's report, the couple willingly accompanied the detectives to police headquarters and spoke openly and without counsel for a couple of hours.

Vicky Miller, who was twenty-seven years old, said she had first met "T" (as she referred to Thompson throughout the interview) about five years earlier, when she had testified in a divorce suit for a friend he was representing. Less than a year after that meeting, she contacted him for help with the divorce of her own husband at the time, Robert Larson, but, wrote Blakely, Thompson's "fee was too high so she decided against [the divorce]." The following year she got a court order against Larson, had him removed from her home, and went back to see Thompson. "The middle of the next week, 'T' called and asked her to go out for dinner," Blakely noted. "She refused and said she was going out with her girlfriends. Later that night they met him at the Manor [a restaurant and bar on West Seventh Street]. He gave her a ride home." A week later, Thompson called her again. He asked her to dinner, and she accepted. "She began to like him more and more," and began seeing him first once and then twice a week.

Mrs. Miller told the detectives that Thompson took her on business trips to northern Minnesota, and that on at least one such trip, they had spent the night together in a motel. On another occasion, she met Thompson in Chicago. Thompson, she said, had reserved two rooms at the Arlington Hotel, but they used only one of them, and after their assignation returned to St. Paul on the train.

Throughout 1961 the lovers trysted frequently, she said. She provided the names of several Twin Cities restaurants, nightspots, and hotels where they enjoyed each other's company. From September 1961 until early 1962, she said, she worked in Thompson's office ("hrs. 9–4") and "dated" him steadily. She said they went out for the last time in January or February 1962. More than a year later, about a week before Carol Thompson's murder, she took a friend to Thompson's office to talk about the friend's divorce. She told Blakely she had not seen or heard from Thompson since.

Michael Miller, Vicky's husband, told Blakely that he "dislike[d] 'T' very much and probably would knock his head off if he met him in an alley." Miller said Thompson had called Vicky frequently since the Millers married in June 1962. On one occasion, Thompson had offered to lend the newlyweds money to buy a house, but, Miller said, he refused the offer and hung up. Miller also told Blakely that in November 1962, he had called the Thompson home and spoke to Carol, informing her of her husband's extramarital activity and demanding that she tell "T" to stay away from his wife—or else. Miller added, however, that "Carol did not seem surprised" by his call and "laughed off" the information.

Miller said he had spent the entire day of March 6 at his job at an East Side market, which his boss later confirmed. Vicky had been at her current job—as a stenographer at an industrial company in downtown St. Paul—the morning of the murder.

The Millers told Blakely, however, that Donald Kelly, "T"'s officemate, had contacted Vicky the day after Carol's death, drove her home after work, and asked where her husband was on the morning of March 6. Vicky, meanwhile, had talked to Thompson's secretary, Kathleen Zajacz, who told her that she had been surprised when "T" arrived at the office so early on the sixth, because he usually showed up, according to Zajacz, between ten and ten-thirty. "Wasn't it awful he came in early *that* day?" Vicky recalled Zajacz saying to her.

The police would talk to Victoria Miller several times during the next several months, and interview her husbands, coworkers, and acquaintances around the country. In the first few days after Carol's murder, the names of several other women, from hatcheck girls to the widows of purported underworld figures, would also be linked with Thompson's. Informants would allege illegitimate children and tell stories of hanky-panky in unlikely places. But if investigators were looking for the archetypical "other woman" to put the lie to the church-going, family-loving persona described by the Thompsons' friends and neighbors, they could hardly have done better than Vicky Miller.

8.

On Saturday, March 9, Carol Thompson's remains were interred at Forest Lawn Cemetery in Maplewood, a quiet, tree-lined suburb on the northern edge of St. Paul.

The interment followed a private funeral service at Edgcumbe Presbyterian attended only by family members and close friends, and officiated by William Paden. T. Eugene had initially decided to have his wife's body cremated, but Doug Young and others talked him out of it, arguing that, under the circumstances, cremation would strike some people as suspicious. Because of the body's condition, the casket was kept closed during the service. And because of the enormous public curiosity, there had been no formal announcement of the rites, no public visitation at the Listoe-Wold Funeral Home on Snelling Avenue prior to the service, and no formal procession from the church to the cemetery. Even so, detectives kept an eye on guests and other callers before the service, and, afterward, the leather-bound book containing the names of the mourners was carefully reviewed by Lieutenant Barkley.

As it happened, one of the most poignant eulogies to Carol Thompson was articulated by Barkley himself, in an interview with Don Giese, a few days after the service. "This woman was one in a million," said the homicide chief, a dour cop in his middle fifties not known for either sentiment or hyperbole. "She simply had no enemies. There was not even the remotest hint that she was anything but a devoted, happy, thoughtful mother and wife. Usually you can find something that might prove useful [to an investigation]—an old boyfriend, an argument, a long-standing grudge, a romance—but this was not [an] average woman. This was a remarkable woman.

"We checked and rechecked. The answer was always the same. If Carol Thompson had done anything to bring about her death, it was beyond any of the information we had about her, and we went back a long, long way. She is dead and she didn't leave behind one clue, one hint, or one faint suggestion of why she is dead."

9.

The frustration in Barkley's remarks was almost palpable. Who would murder a woman such as Carol Thompson? *Why?*

A botched burglary or revenge on the part of a disgruntled client seemed a less plausible explanation with each passing day, and the autopsy had revealed no evidence of a sexual assault. But Barkley, quickly aware of the $1.1 million accidental-death policies on Mrs. Thompson and the rumors of Mr. Thompson's extramarital affairs, surely had a suspect in mind. And though the victim may not have left a clue at the scene, the killer had: most notably, the broken pieces of the pistol grip that investigators found during their initial inspection of the Thompson home. Barkley's task would be to use those clues to connect the suspect and the actual killer, whom he had reason to believe were *not* one and the same.

Under intense pressure from a fearful public and outraged elected officials, metro area police had rounded up dozens of suspicious characters during the first few days after the murder. Abusive husbands and violent boyfriends were reported by wives, lovers, in-laws, and neighbors. Known burglars, housebreakers, peeping Toms, and violent sex offenders were tracked down and hauled in for interrogation, though most were quickly released. Transients, drunks, mentally ill and disabled persons—men of various ages and circumstances who looked or behaved peculiarly in another citizen's eyes—were checked out as well. A man who had been imprisoned for sex crimes in Nebraska and another man who had walked uninvited into several St. Paul homes in the days surrounding the Thompson murder were apprehended and given a particularly close examination. Nonetheless, it is highly probable that, in Barkley's mind, Cotton Thompson was the only credible suspect from the beginning.

Two days after the murder, Barkley requested his first meeting with Thompson. For two hours on Friday afternoon, March 8, Thompson, red-eyed, solemn, and accompanied by Donald Kelly, answered the investigator's questions about clients, acquaintances, and possible motives. Thompson again said he could think of no one besides, presumably, the aforementioned Kenneth Moran, whose alibi had been confirmed, and no reason why someone would want to murder his wife. Again he vowed to do everything in his power to help identify the murderer or murderers.

For several days after that initial interview, neither Barkley nor Thompson said anything substantive for publication. Reporters found themselves caught between an official policy of silence and the myriad rumors swirling around them. Even the tireless Don Giese could do little but describe his attempts to draw information from Barkley and Thompson, repeat the inevitable *No comment* responses, and leave the unconfirmed reports regarding insurance policies, other women, and underworld connections unpublished. Barkley and his men were working extended shifts. Thompson and his children, assisted by his oldest sister, Mrs. Freeman Gesche, a farmer's wife from Blue Earth, had moved back into 1720 Hillcrest after friends had thoroughly cleaned the house and painters had redone portions of the walls and woodwork. To the surprise of many of those friends and neighbors, the day after the murder Thompson had returned to work and the children had been sent back to school. Thompson and the Swobodas had decided to carry on as "normally as possible," in Mrs. Gesche's words, during the difficult days that followed Carol's death.

For the next two weeks there was little fresh, substantiated news. Then, on March 22, fourteen days after their previous interview, Barkley wondered aloud, and for publication, why Thompson had not been in touch with him and, for that matter, had ignored Barkley's requests for further talks. In an obvious allusion to both the rumors and Cotton's apparent immersion in his work, the investigator remarked wryly, "Perhaps if Mr. Thompson could find time to drop in for a conference, we could get some things straightened out. We have a lot to talk to him about." But Thompson did not respond.

Finally, on March 26, the widower issued his first extended public comment. In a six-and-a-half-page typed statement distributed to the media by Doug Young, Thompson laid out a "brief synopsis" of the family's life-insurance holdings and four other topics of presumed interest to the community. Young was, by this time, a familiar—and credible—name in the case. A World War II combat veteran, he was several years older than Cotton, but he and his wife had known the Thompsons since their school days at Macalester and were close friends of the family. Though not a lawyer himself,

Young was, at the time of Carol's murder, the Republican Party's executive secretary in Ramsey County and well-connected within St. Paul's political, legal, and law enforcement communities.

In the first section of the statement, Thompson listed the insurance companies with whom he was doing business and the type, cost, amount, and date of purchase of each of the several policies. The policies on Carol's life totaled, as the police had already determined, $1.061 million, the policies on his own "approximately" $460,000. Then, under Roman numerals *II.* through *V.*, he itemized his net worth ($115,000), summarized the family's income for the years 1960 through 1962 ("total joint gross income from all sources . . ." in 1962: $44,693), enumerated "major trips" that he and Carol had taken in 1962 and 1963, and described the couple's recent home decoration that left them no choice but to give away the "never properly train[ed]" dachshund that he had purchased from a neighbor three years earlier. Under numeral *VI.*, the statement concluded: "I hope that this information will correct the fanciful, far-fetched stories that some people have been alluding to. I have requested an appointment with a law enforcement official to again go over this material, and to again answer any questions relative to my personal life that might be asked, and to again discuss the clients that I have had in the past within the bounds of legal ethics."

But instead of correcting misconceptions, Thompson's prolix statement added fuel to the rumors and increased the public's demands for official action. Barkley was furious. He told Giese that he thought Thompson was trying to force investigators to arrest him before they had a solid case. "Then he could go running up to the Supreme Court, screaming for immediate trial," the homicide commander said. If that was indeed Thompson's plan, Barkley continued, he would be happy to disappoint him. He vowed to hold off on any arrest until he was ready.

On March 29, at the widower's request, Thompson met again with the homicide commander at police headquarters. This time, Thompson brought along Young, Paden, and a hired stenographer to record the conversation. Barkley, who was joined by Ramsey County Attorney Bill Randall, asked most of the questions, retracing now-familiar ground: the huge life insurance purchases, the absent dog, Thompson's extramarital interests, and his actions on March 6. The meeting reportedly lasted for more than four hours, but yielded nothing that Barkley did not already know.

10.

A month passed. Minnesota's famously long winter mellowed into a typically tentative spring. But, whatever and whomever Barkley and his investigators suspected, there was still no compelling reason to book anyone for Carol Thompson's murder.

T. Eugene had resumed his normal activities, moving back and forth between his home and his downtown office, attending bar association meetings, and showing up at various Twin Cities restaurants and clubs—suddenly one of the most readily recognized, most talked about persons in town. Some reports described him as uncharacteristically withdrawn, hollow-eyed, and shrunken on his diminutive frame. But others said that he was as outgoing and brash as ever. Giese later related a brief but memorable example of the latter version. Two days after the murder, Cotton—a drink in hand—walked up to Mayor George Vavoulis at the St. Paul Athletic Club and announced, "I'm Thompson," apparently believing he needed no additional introduction and, in any case, was someone the mayor would be eager to meet. "I never could understand why he introduced himself to me and offered to buy me a drink at a time like that," Vavoulis told Giese. "I'd never met him before in my life."

Thompson continued to enjoy the support of close friends and associates, though he would sometimes, usually after a couple of drinks, put them on the spot by plaintively asking, "Do you think I really did this?" Presumably, they told him they did not. More important, they seemed to be unanimous in their statements to police, telling investigators that they could not imagine Cotton being involved in Carol's death. By all appearances, they insisted, the Thompsons had been a happy couple. "When the two of them did have an argument," Marian Erickson told Detective Willinger, "they were the kind who would shout at each other and even throw things, thereby getting it out of their systems, holding no grudge."

Thompson's children, often in the care of their aunts and grandparents, went to school and played with friends, presenting a much lower profile than their father. They were nonetheless the object of widespread interest. Most of the attention was confined to the neighborhood and their schools, where the children were treated with kindness and sympathy by their teachers, friends, and friends' parents. The cars of curious strangers—often brandishing Instamatic and Brownie cameras—still crept past the Thompson house on the odd chance their occupants would catch a glimpse of a family member coming or going, but the traffic on Hillcrest was not bumper-to-bumper the way it had been the first few days after the murder. And the media, rebuffed by Mr. Thompson, most of his close friends, and relatives, maintained a hands-off policy with the youngsters, their teachers, and their playmates. (Apparently, the first published photo of the children appeared in *The Saturday Evening Post* a full six months after the murder.) So, it would seem, did Barkley, who probably felt that his detectives, during their brief conversations on the afternoon of March 6, had obtained as much information as the children were able to provide.

In the reports from that period, there are, though, enough separate references to Jeff Thompson and his sisters—as opposed to the frequent collective mention of "Carol and the children" and "the Thompson kids"—to remind a reader that several individual lives were caught in the cat-and-mouse game that had ensued between the police and their father. In a follow-up interview with investigators a few weeks after the murder, for instance, Kenneth Moran, while giving his impressions of the Thompson children, told Barkley that "T" favored Patty, Margaret lacked "spunk," Amy was "sickly" and "underweight," and Jeff was a "sensitive boy" whom Moran once took hunting with his own sons. (Years later, Jeff would have no recollection of that hunting trip.) On another occasion, the Thompsons' next-door neighbor, Merlyn Erikson, said Patty reported that a schoolmate "had made the remark that her Daddy is a murderer."

Finally, in a March 25 report, Detective Blakely reported this brief encounter at 1720 Hillcrest:

> I pushed the front doorbell and a boy answered. He said, "Dad isn't home." I asked when [his father] would be home and he [said he] did not know. I asked who he was and he said, "Jeff." I asked if he would tell his father [that] Lieutenant Barkley would like to see him in his office. He said he would tell him and I left.

11.

On April 5, George Barkley again turned to the public for help. At a televised press conference, he and St. Paul Police Chief Lester McAuliffe displayed the fragments of the pistol grip found at the crime scene. The grip, which fit a standard 7.65-millimeter Luger, was apparently one of a kind—a handcrafted black and white plastic laminate. The investigators hoped the grip was unusual enough that someone would recognize it and tell them something about the weapon to which it belonged.

Pictures of the grip fragments and a Luger like the one the police were seeking appeared on the evening newscasts and the front pages of Twin Cities papers. Four days later, a traveling salesman named Wayne Brandt called the police. Brandt said that he had made the handle for his Luger in a vocational shop class. The Luger had been stolen during a burglary of his south Minneapolis apartment on February 14, less than three weeks before Carol Thompson's murder.

The next break came on April 17, when two Twin Cities men were arrested on suspicion of holding up a St. Paul bar on April 8. Henry Butler, twenty-eight, and Willard Ingram, thirty-five, were local roofers who supplemented their legitimate income with small-time crime, or vice versa. Confronted with attempted robbery and assault charges (one of the robbers had slugged the bookkeeper during the holdup at the Trade Winds tavern), Ingram, who had already spent nearly half his life in jail, decided to come clean in hopes of striking a deal with the county attorney. He confessed to the burglary of several area businesses and residences, including Wayne Brandt's Minneapolis apartment. Ingram said that he, Butler, and a third man, Richard Sharp, had taken a television set, a box of coins, and the much-discussed Luger during a daytime break-in of Brandt's flat, and stashed the loot at Sharp's house in north Minneapolis.

Barkley was notified immediately. When the homicide boss walked into Ingram's holding cell and brought up the subject of Carol Thompson's murder, Ingram was even more forthcoming. By the time he and Butler stopped talking, investigators had learned that the burglars had passed the stolen Luger to another man, a one-time prizefighter named Norman Mastrian, in the presence of Dick Sharp and a third man, Sheldon Morris, about two weeks before the Thompson murder. Butler said he saw Mastrian hand the pistol to yet another man, Dick Anderson, the day before the slaying. According to Butler, who was as desperate as Ingram to avoid murder charges, Anderson and Sharp had fled the Twin

Cities for Arizona when the photos of the Luger and the handle fragments appeared in the papers.

Barkley recognized a couple of the names. Sharp had been mentioned in one of the anonymous tips alleging T. Eugene's philandering. More interesting yet, Barkley recalled that Mastrian had been a suspect in the unsolved 1961 execution-style murder of a shady St. Paul restaurateur named Eddie James—and that Mastrian's attorneys at the time included Thompson. Dick Anderson was an unfamiliar name to Barkley, but not to police in Minneapolis and Hennepin County, where Anderson, like Ingram, Butler, Morris, and Sharp, had been in trouble with the law. None of the men, except Mastrian, was known or suspected to have been involved in murder; their offenses had been limited, as far as investigators knew, to robbery, burglary, possession of stolen property, and transporting stolen autos across state lines. But Barkley, after comparing notes with his counterparts on the west side of the river, had learned enough to act.

On April 19, Barkley's men arrested Mastrian at his north suburban Spring Lake Park home. A darkly handsome native of Duluth, Minnesota, a Navy veteran, and yet another alumnus of Macalester College, Mastrian reportedly boasted an I.Q. of one hundred and fifty. He was forty, married, and the father of two children. He offered no resistance when the police kicked in his door and took him downtown, where he was photographed by the press wearing dark glasses and puffing on a long cigar. The same day, police in Phoenix separately arrested Anderson and Sharp, also without incident. Inadvertently tipped off by an over-eager Minneapolis newsman who had learned of his whereabouts in Arizona, Anderson was checking out of the Tropics Motel when Phoenix police officers walked into the lobby and recognized him from the description forwarded from Minnesota. Morris, aware of the arrests in both states, turned himself in to St. Paul police on April 22.

Across the Twin Cities, residents greeted the news of the arrests—a dramatic breakthrough in the six-week investigation—with excitement and relief.

Among the statements to the media on April 19 was a typed, two-paragraph "release" from the office of T. Eugene Thompson. The statement read:

> I am very pleased with the news this morning from the St. Paul Police Department and the County Attorney's office that important new developments have taken place concerning the solution of my wife's murder. I pray that the guilty parties will be quickly brought to justice.
>
> I telephoned the County Attorney, William Randall, this morning and congratulated him on the good news. I again assured him of my fullest cooperation in the solution of this brutal crime.

12.

On Saturday, April 20, the morning after his arrest, Dick Anderson sat in an interrogation room at Phoenix police headquarters with two detectives recently arrived from the Twin Cities.

The suspect, who gave his full name as Dick W.C. Anderson (he said the middle initials stood alone, not signifying middle names), was a handsome man of middling height and build, with green eyes and brown hair, casually dressed in a sport coat and slacks—a man in no way out of the ordinary in his physical appearance or attire. He was thirty-five years old, he had told the Phoenix police, a native of Alden, Michigan, who currently resided in Minneapolis. An honorably discharged Marine Corps sergeant with a Purple Heart for shrapnel wounds received in Korea, he was married but separated from his wife, who lived in Michigan. A report sent to police from Marine headquarters also revealed that, despite the honorable discharge, in his almost seven years with the corps he had been reprimanded three times—for neglect of duties, being absent without official leave, and drinking while on guard duty. Though eligible for partial-disability payments as the result of his injuries, for the past couple of years he had made his living selling roofing and siding for a Minneapolis-based home-improvement company. He was in Arizona, he said, on vacation.

Detectives Larry McMullen of the Hennepin County sheriff's department in Minneapolis and Gerald Bodin of St. Paul's homicide squad had, however, more up-to-date information, some of which had come from the robbers Willard Ingram and Henry Butler in Minnesota and some of which the detectives had learned from fellow fugitive Dick Sharp, whom they had interviewed earlier in the Phoenix jail. McMullen, who knew Anderson from the latter's scrapes with police in the Twin Cities, proceeded to enumerate that information to the suspect. Ingram, Butler, and Norman Mastrian were in custody in St. Paul, and Sharp had just been interviewed in Phoenix, McMullen told Anderson. "We know that Mastrian hired you to kill Mrs. Thompson, and that you were promised $3,000 to do the job," the detective said. "We know that you received a stolen Luger automatic from Dick Sharp, and that, when the gun wouldn't fire, you beat Mrs. Thompson with the weapon and then stabbed her in the throat with a paring knife you found in her kitchen."

McMullen paused to let his words sink in, then asked the suspect if the information was correct.

Anderson was silent for a moment before agreeing that it was. "What kind of deal can I get if I go back there and cooperate with you people?" he asked.

There won't be any deals, McMullen told him.

Nonetheless, against the advice of a Phoenix attorney, Anderson decided to waive extradition. Escorted by McMullen, he was flown back to Minnesota on April 26. George Barkley was waiting when their Western Airlines flight arrived at Wold Chamberlain Field in the Twin Cities.

In St. Paul, William Randall, the Ramsey County attorney, filed first-degree murder charges against Mastrian and Anderson. Bail for each man was set at $100,000, the highest to date in Minnesota history.

On April 30, a grand jury was convened, as required by state law, to consider first-degree murder indictments. Among the grand jury's witnesses over the next several days of secret proceedings was T. Eugene Thompson, who appeared voluntarily and testified for more than six hours before leaving on the advice of his newly hired counsel, St. Paul defense attorneys Hyam Segell and William Fallon.

Also on April 30, several investigators accompanied Sheldon Morris to the rural community of Elk River, about thirty minutes north of the Twin Cities. There, after searching for several hours in the swampy terrain, the officers located a rusted Luger pistol with a missing handle grip. Morris had told the police that shortly before noon on March 6, on Norman Mastrian's instructions, he had driven Mastrian and Anderson to the area, where the men tossed the gun into the weeds and discarded several articles of clothing that Anderson had brought along in a pillow case and cut into small pieces as they drove. The investigators sealed the rusty Luger in a plastic bag and took it to the police department's crime lab in St. Paul, where it was immediately examined by Ted Elzerman and his staff. The following day, in his report to Barkley, the criminalist noted that the Luger had been "subjected to considerable abuse." The trigger guard and handle-grip frame were bent out of shape, and the magazine had been jammed into the handle with enough force to knock off both of its ejection knobs. What is more, "the portion of a white/black/white grip recovered . . . in the Master Bedroom at 1720 Hillcrest was compared to the missing toe of the left grip plate and found to fit mechanically."

A short time later, when searchers returned to the swampy area north of town, they found cut-up pieces of a pair of blood-stained trousers a few miles from where the Luger had been recovered. The name ANDERSON was printed on one of the trouser remnants.

Meanwhile, the hapless Trade Winds robbers, still worried about homicide charges, continued to talk to police. In a jailhouse conversation with Detective Bodin on May 6, Ingram described the break-in at Wayne Brandt's apartment and the attempts to sell the stolen Luger during the following couple of days. When they couldn't peddle the gun, Ingram said, Sharp decided to keep it. A few days after that, Ingram continued, he sat alongside Sharp in the back seat of a convertible outside the Big Dipper Bar near downtown Minneapolis. Sharp introduced him to Mastrian and Morris, who were seated in front.

After some small talk, Ingram told Bodin, Mastrian asked him if he would like to make a couple of thousand dollars.

"Doing what?" Ingram said.

"We want a broad knocked off," Mastrian replied.

"What for?"

"Oh, either for a will or some insurance, or something like that."

Ingram asked who the woman was—"a tramp or a drunk or someone like that?"

"No," Mastrian said, in Ingram's account. "She doesn't smoke or drink, and she's a churchgoer."

When Ingram asked about the woman's family, Mastrian said that she had three or four kids.

Ingram told Bodin that he made it clear he was not interested. ("I don't do things like that.") He said he later found out that Mastrian had previously offered the job to Sharp, who had likewise turned it down.

Ingram said he was stunned to learn about Carol Thompson's murder. "I came home one evening and I picked up the newspaper and I read about this woman being murdered," he said. Reading about the victim's children and church membership, "I realized this was actually the woman I was propositioned to kill." Then, two days after the murder, he told Bodin, he went to Sharp's house for a drink. Present along with Sharp's wife and a handful of other people was Dick Anderson, whom Ingram said he knew casually and who, a month or two earlier, had asked him to come along on a restaurant robbery that apparently never occurred. On this particular evening, Anderson was drinking heavily.

Sitting beside him on Sharp's sofa, Ingram recalled, Anderson turned and said, "I never saw anybody who wanted to live so hard in all my life." Spooked by the comment, Ingram told Anderson that he had better forget about it, to which Anderson replied, "Yeah, I guess I better. But, jeez, I just can't get over how I had to kill her."

Despite Ingram's self-described nervous protests, Anderson kept talking, resuming the monologue an hour or two later, when the two men stopped at a Washington Avenue tavern for a nightcap. Seated some distance from the other customers at the bar, Anderson described in extensive detail how he had killed the woman, first clubbing her with the defective pistol, then stabbing her with a paring knife he had pulled out of a kitchen drawer. Anderson could not believe, Ingram said, that "she could take that much punishment."

Bodin asked Ingram if Carol Thompson's name was mentioned in the discussion he had with Mastrian and Morris prior to the murder.

"Never," Ingram replied.

"Was Mr. Thompson's name ever mentioned?" Bodin asked.

"No," Ingram said. All he knew about the Thompsons was what he read in the paper after the murder.

On Wednesday, May 8, two months after the killing, the Ramsey County grand jury indicted Norman Mastrian and Dick Anderson on charges of murder in the first degree. The grand jury also decided that Sheldon Morris should face charges of being an accessory after the fact. George Barkley publicly declared the case "two-thirds solved."

13.

Following the indictments, the major players in the Thompson case chose to keep quiet. Mastrian and his attorneys decided to seek as many delays en route to trial as possible, in the meantime saying nothing about the case to investigators. Anderson, on the advice, first, of his Phoenix lawyer and then of St. Paul Public Defender Thomas Moore, said nothing further to detectives, pending what he hoped would be a reduction in charges from first- to second-degree murder in exchange for his cooperation. T. Eugene Thompson—unindicted by the grand jury but more isolated than ever under a lowering cloud of suspicion—continued to refuse either public comment or further discussion with Barkley and Randall. The latter, for his part, was unwilling to discuss a deal with Moore, no doubt believing that Ingram, Butler, and Sharp had given him as much leverage as he needed for the moment and that, more likely sooner than later, one of the indicted men—the best bet was Anderson—would break under the pressure.

Neither Mastrian nor Anderson could make the $100,000 bail, and they remained under close watch in the Ramsey County jail. Thompson had vacated his Minnesota Building office and was working out of his home, his whereabouts and activities monitored by Barkley's detectives, insurance company investigators, Twin Cities reporters, and, with increasing uneasiness, his own friends and neighbors.

One of Thompson's neighbors told Detective Willinger that Cotton appeared "to be back to his normal, 'cocky' manner and habits." "He felt that he had beaten Randall," Willinger quoted the neighbor as saying. Other neighbors said that "strange men"—clients, perhaps, or out-of-town acquaintances—would stop by and sometimes spend the night. On at least one occasion, a "pretty woman" arrived by taxi cab, according to Willinger's informant, and the Thompson children were "locked out of the house for an hour."

A female acquaintance said that Thompson had asked her out to dinner, explaining that he had lost weight since his wife's death, presumably because he hated to dine alone. To the woman's surprise and bemusement ("Maybe I took it wrong," she told Detective Bodin), Thompson noted, "Now I'm a single man, and it's no holds barred." The woman said she turned him down and had not spoken to him since. Another woman said Thompson had invited her to the Hillcrest house and tearfully discussed, among other topics, Vicky Miller and possible suspects in his wife's murder. He insisted that he was innocent, the woman said, but conceded that the public was convinced otherwise. She told Detective Blakely that if Thompson *was* guilty, he was "a good actor."

On the evening of June 14, Detectives Blakely and Williams ran into Thompson at LaNasa's, a Snelling Avenue bar popular with St. Paul lawyers, cops, and newspapermen. Thompson, who had been sitting at a table with two men, walked over to the detectives at the bar and, with typical chutzpah, said (according to Williams), "I don't care if you're embarrassed or not, I'm going to say hello to you, Ernie." The threesome had a "conversation of a non-pertinent nature," in Williams' words, and Thompson bought the investigators a drink.

Less than a week later, the glass wall that had been shielding Thompson suddenly cracked and shattered.

Beset by nightmares and alcohol-withdrawal pangs, Anderson was frustrated and frightened by Randall's refusal to reduce the charges against him. On June 20, after conferring with Larry Mc-Mullen, the Hennepin County detective who had brought him back from Arizona, he decided to disregard his lawyer's advice and tell investigators everything he knew. That evening, after announcing his intention to talk, he was whisked to the Ramsey County sheriff's office in the St. Paul courthouse, where he was closeted with Barkley, McMullen, and a police stenographer named George Galles.

For the next two hours—of his "own free will, without threats, promises, or inducements being made . . . by any member of the St. Paul police department," in Barkley's prefatory language—Anderson talked.

Chain-smoking and sweating profusely, according to later reports, Anderson answered the investigators' questions in precise, specific terms. He began with a simple declaration: "I killed Mrs. Carol Thompson." He did so, he said, at the victim's home, at 1720 Hillcrest Avenue in St. Paul, shortly after eight-thirty on the morning of March 6. No one else was present. Then he recounted his March 3 introduction to Norman Mastrian by Richard Sharp, and conversations with Mastrian that evening and the next day. "[Mastrian] said that the woman that was to be killed was a criminal attorney's wife," Anderson said. "He said the name was Thompson. He asked me if I had ever heard of him. I said, 'No.'" He said Mastrian would pay him $4,000 if he made the murder look like an accident, or $2,000 if he did not. Ultimately, Anderson said, he and Mastrian agreed to split the difference: "I would take $3,000, accident or no accident." He said Mastrian gave him a $200 down payment, which, Mastrian told him, "was all [he] could raise on such a short notice."

Anderson told about meeting with Mastrian on March 4, when the two of them drove around the Thompsons' block in Highland Park and, over coffee a short time later, Mastrian drew floor plans of the Thompson house on a napkin. According to the plan, Anderson said, he would surprise Mrs. Thompson the next morning, after her husband and children had left the house, when she answered her husband's telephone call in the kitchen. Anderson would knock her unconscious with a thick rubber "whopper" that Mastrian had provided, submerge her in her bathtub, and, applying "reverse artificial respiration," cause her to drown. He said he was supposed to kill the woman on the morning of March 5, but had "chickened out" and stayed in bed. Later that morning, Mastrian had called and asked what happened. Anderson told him that the bookkeeper at work had gotten sick and he had had to fill in. He also told Mastrian he needed a gun, and, later that day, Mastrian (not Dick Sharp) had given him the Luger. Finally, on the morning of the sixth, fortified by vodka and amphetamines and wearing a tie and a sport jacket under his coat, he had driven the eight miles from his south Minneapolis apartment through the pre-dawn dark to Highland Park, entered the Thompson house through the unlocked side door, waited in the basement while the woman's family dressed, ate, and departed for work and school, then climbed the basement stairs, proceeded to the master bedroom on the second floor, and confronted her as she read a magazine in bed.

The fact that almost nothing came off according to plan, that what was supposed to look like a bathroom accident turned into a literal bloodbath, did not negate the existence of a plan, with its bizarre echo of *Dial M for Murder*, the Alfred Hitchcock thriller of a few years earlier. And Anderson made it clear that in setting the stage for the plan's execution, T. Eugene Thompson—whom he had never met, he said, but had learned of from Mastrian—had gotten rid of the family dog, removed a telephone extension from the master bedroom, made sure the side door was unlocked, and called home from his office in order to draw Carol to the kitchen phone (now the only phone in the house), where Anderson was supposed to knock her out with the blackjack-like "whopper." Anderson explained that the stairs had squeaked when he had gone down the basement and he was afraid that Mrs. Thompson would hear him coming, so, improvising on the plan, he waited until she had gone back up to the bedroom before surprising her. He described the beating and stabbing, followed by his victim's unlikely escape and his own departure from the house.

Finally, he described returning to his Minneapolis apartment, talking to Mastrian on the phone, then driving north of the city with Mastrian and Shelly Morris to dispose of the broken Luger and his bloody clothes. He said that he eventually received two more payments, totaling $2,100 and delivered by Morris.

"I am very sorry that the whole thing happened and I wish it hadn't," he concluded.

At twenty minutes after midnight, on the morning of June 21, Anderson signed a hurriedly typed, twenty-page transcription of his confession. "Now maybe I can get some sleep," he murmured.

Moments later, municipal court judge J. Clifford Janes signed a warrant for T. Eugene Thompson's arrest on suspicion of first-degree murder.

14.

While Dick Anderson was taken back to his cell, a task force of detectives from state, county, and city law-enforcement agencies, assembled by George Barkley and accompanied by Doug Young, drove up Highway 61 from St. Paul to the Thompsons' cottage on the north shore of Forest Lake.

The cottage was a comfortable, well-equipped, but unpretentious place owned by Otto and Toni Swoboda. For several years the Swobodas had shared it with Cotton, Carol, and the kids, who called it, somewhat grandly, their "summer home" and spent weeks at a time at the property. Like many Twin Citians, the Thompsons considered a lake place an integral part of their Minnesota way of life. Many of the children's pals headed "up north" with their families when school let out for the season. The Thompson kids were luckier than most, though, because "up north" for them was only an hour from home, which meant weekend and even day trips were common. After Carol's death, the site functioned as a hideaway. Though its location was quickly known by the police, media, and some of the case's more aggressive followers, the cabin was far enough off the beaten track to be inconvenient for the casually nosy.

During the summer, T. Eugene commuted between Forest Lake and St. Paul, where he saw clients, consulted with his attorneys, and, despite the ongoing investigation, maintained a busy social life. The Swobodas came and went. Otto had a business to run in St. Paul, and Toni preferred the ordered tranquility of her city home to a cabin full of grandkids, even—perhaps especially—in the aftermath of her daughter's murder. In any event, the Thompson children, who often were allowed to bring playmates to the cabin, were usually supervised by Alta Grassinger, the housekeeper hired after the murder by their father and granddad, or an aunt or older cousin.

There was hardly any traffic in the sultry wee hours of June 21, and Barkley's posse made the trip in scarcely half an hour. But when they arrived at the cottage, Thompson had not yet returned for the night from St. Paul. The children were sleeping, according to their cousin and temporary nanny, Sharon Gesche, who let the detectives in, and the Swobodas were at home in the city. The detectives said they would wait.

Thompson arrived about an hour later. Despite the muggy heat, he was dressed in a crisp summer suit, tab-collar shirt, color-coordinated tie and breast-pocket handkerchief, and straw fedora. Entering the silent cottage, he locked the door behind him, clearly not expecting company and no doubt surprised to find Barkley's men waiting for him. He did not resist when Detective Earl Miels told him he was under arrest for his wife's murder. The officers gave him permission to wash up and change his shirt, but denied his request to wake the kids.

Thompson did not argue. Calmly, the way a mildly exasperated citizen might wonder aloud about some bureaucratic folderol, he merely asked the detectives, "Why is this necessary? I would have come in if you wanted me."

That This Man Was a Monster

1.

Back in St. Paul, T. Eugene Thompson was charged with first-degree murder in the death of his wife, though, as he had done since he was first discussed as a suspect more than three months earlier, he insisted he had nothing to do with the crime.

Following his arrest, Thompson was photographed for the conventional mug shots—Prisoner I.D. # 52024, in a dark suit and white tab-collar shirt sans necktie—and arraigned in St. Paul municipal court. On June 25, he was indicted by the Ramsey County grand jury. Later, walking out of the Ramsey County jail after posting his $100,000 bail, he was greeted by dozens of reporters. When one of them shouted, "What are you going to tell your kids?" he replied evenly, "I'm going to tell them the truth."

During the next several months, Thompson's attorneys, Hy

Segell and Bill Fallon, flooded the courts with pretrial motions, asking for various forms of relief, from suppressing evidence removed from the Thompson home by police on the day of the murder (including the pistol grip fragments and thirty-caliber bullets, as well as police photos of the bloody front hallway) to dismissing all charges against him. Segell, who was forty, and Fallon, then thirty-one, were former federal prosecutors who were well-connected and respected in the Twin Cities. Both had known Thompson casually before the murder. "St. Paul was a small town, with only about six hundred lawyers at the time, so we all kind of knew each other," Fallon said later. Thompson, however, stood out—a "distinctive character," in Fallon's words.

The serial motions bought the defense some time, but, all things considered, not much else. By the end of that summer, all but one of the motions had been denied. That one, requesting a change of trial venue—to Hennepin County (Minneapolis) from Ramsey County (St. Paul), where, according to the motion, the daily papers and rampant gossip had "poisoned the minds of the community"—had been rejected by a district court; but Segell and Fallon had appealed, and, on September 13, the lower court's ruling was overturned by the state supreme court. Changes of venue, though not unheard of in the United States, were still rare at the time. In any event, Thompson's lawyers seemed to believe that a move across the river—to the larger, purportedly more cosmopolitan, less gossip-fueled twin, as opposed to, say, more distant Rochester, Duluth, or Moorhead—would enhance their client's chances.

As it happened, the daily papers, as full of Thompson-related articles as they were during the summer and early fall, told only part of the so-called "real" stories that were making their way through the Twin Cities at the time. The local rumor mills were running full steam prior to the trial, keeping investigators and journalists busy checking out even the most preposterous "leads." There were unsubstantiated reports, for example, of unnamed children fathered by T. Eugene, paternity suits, abortions, gambling debts, "Mob" relationships, and a "gang" attempt to blackmail the Swobodas, as well as frequent, though also unsubstantiated, sightings of the significant figures in various combinations and settings, including one report that had Carol Thompson partying with Mastrian and Anderson in rural Wisconsin.

For the police, the respective attorneys, and the community at large, it was thus quite probably a relief when the trial finally began on a chilly fall morning, in the old, fortress-like municipal courthouse in downtown Minneapolis, with Hennepin County District Court Judge Rolf Fosseen presiding.

2.

State of Minnesota v. Tilmer Eugene Thompson was advertised and described as "the trial of the century" in Minnesota, a reasonable claim when it began on October 28, 1963, and long afterward as well. A widely admired and much-loved mother of four small children had been brutally murdered in her own home in a fashionable, presumably safe neighborhood of a law-abiding community. An upward-bound attorney, husband, and father was on trial for his life.

"It had everything," lead prosecutor William Randall said nearly four decades later, referring to the essential components of a classic murder case. "Blood, money, and sex." He added: "Murders were relatively rare in the Twin Cities then. And this one was unsolved for some time, which made it doubly rare."

Randall had pieced together the state's case over the previous several months, but he had not expected to try it. As county attorney, he had positioned himself as an administrator, not a litigator.

"I don't intend to try cases," he explained during his election campaign in 1962. "I intend to be the boss." At forty-seven, he was a smart, congenial, phlegmatic man whose disheveled mop of dark hair, lined face, and lanky physique frequently evoked comparisons with Abraham Lincoln—which, as an occasional Republican Party office-seeker, he did not go out of his way to discourage. He had grown up in the verdant Town & Country neighborhood of St. Paul, on a block not dissimilar from Hillcrest Avenue in Highland Park. He was described as a dedicated family man who enjoyed spending time with his wife and children, boating on the Minnesota River, and tending to a Christmas tree farm he owned east of the Twin Cities. Since March 6, however, Carol Thompson's murder had been a near-constant preoccupation, and, since T. Eugene's arrest in June, he had spent eighteen-hour days responding to the Thompson team's motions and preparing for trial. Before Carol Thompson's murder, he had known T. Eugene only by sight, bumping into him at the St. Paul Athletic Club and other downtown hangouts. The only time he had seen Carol was with George Barkley at the Ancker Hospital morgue. The sight of her battered body had been a profound shock, he said years later, and he vowed he would never look at a murder victim again. Meanwhile, the top trial lawyer on his staff, who would probably have tried the Thompson case, had died suddenly of a heart attack, so Randall, with the assistance of the county's first African-American prosecutor, Stephen Maxwell, decided the task was his.

The case continued to be a hot topic of local conversation. According to at least one newspaper survey at the time, T. Eugene Thompson's name was recognized by more than ninety-five percent of Minnesota's population—about the same percentage that knew the name of U.S. Senator Hubert H. Humphrey, then the state's best-known public official, and Minnesota Twins slugger Harmon Killebrew. Inevitably drawing comparisons with the sensational Sam Sheppard and Finch-Tregoff murder cases* of the previous several years, the Thompson trial attracted national, and even international, attention. Reporters from newspapers in New York and Chicago were regulars in Judge Fosseen's courtroom, and the case merited long features in large-circulation magazines. *The Saturday Evening Post* ran a five-page, three-thousand-word piece, written by the *Dispatch*'s Don Giese, in mid-September, anticipating the trial's opening. *Life,* the most popular general-interest magazine in the country at the time, had prepared an extensive feature of its own, but the story was spiked to make room for coverage of President Kennedy's assassination. In fact, a Thompson trial update from Minneapolis was running on United Press International's national news wire at 12:34 PM Central Standard Time on Friday, November 22, when the first bulletin from Dallas interrupted scheduled transmissions.

In the Twin Cities, the Thompson trial was front-page news almost every day from opening gavel to final adjournment almost six weeks later. Beneath banner headlines, multiple accounts of the proceedings trumped most other local, national, and international news, usually running dozens of column inches each day, jumping from the front page and sharing large blocks of the inside pages with ads for Rambler Ambassadors, women's girdles, and $83 Western Airlines "Sunbreaks" to Arizona. Only the president's assassination and state funeral would supersede the trial coverage in the local papers.

On many days during the trial, black-and-white photos in all

* Sam Sheppard and Bernard Finch were prominent surgeons who had been convicted, after highly publicized trials, of first-degree murder in the deaths of their wives—Marilyn Sheppard, in Cleveland, in 1954, and Barbara Finch, in Los Angeles, in 1960. Also convicted in the Finch case was the doctor's mistress, Carole Tregoff. Bill Randall said he studied both cases while preparing for the Thompson trial.

four of the local dailies showed the crowd of curious citizens queued up outside Courtroom 238, waiting for the thirty-five gallery seats available for each session. Wearing or carrying the hats and overcoats that signify the approach of a Minnesota winter, some snacked, others chatted or read, and several hunkered down on blankets and camp stools as though they were waiting for play-off tickets or a Broadway road-show opening. In many of the photos, the kibitzers (perhaps two-thirds of them women, nearly all adults, though running the gamut from school-skipping teens to day-tripping retirees) provided a human backdrop to the trial's major players—the lawyers, witnesses, and defendant himself—as the latter came and went or enjoyed a cigarette break.

Thompson was pictured almost daily, always fastidiously attired in a well-fitted suit and conservative tie, always exhibiting the ramrod posture and thousand-yard gaze of a Marine sentry, never returning, or even seeming to be aware of, the stares of the wide-eyed crowd. Near the end of the trial an unidentified woman holding a small child was photographed as she glared at Thompson when he and one of his attorneys walked past. According to the photo caption, the woman screamed, "Murderer! Fiend!" Thompson's response, if any, was not recorded.

The text of the press coverage was usually voluminous, often including several pages of verbatim testimony or statements. Radio and television equipment was not allowed in the courtroom, but local stations' news shows usually included snippets of black-and-white film of the principals arriving, departing, or smoking during a recess, with a concise voice-over recap of the day's developments. Because the basic story elements were, by now, so familiar, print reporters like Don Giese and J. C. Wolfe of the St. Paul dailies, the *Tribune*'s Al McConagha, and the *Star*'s Barbara Flanagan had the opportunity to paint detailed pictures of the drama's participants. The hair color, body type, suit and necktie choices, voice levels, and demeanors of everyone with a starring role were meticulously described. Fosseen was "tall, rugged, broad-shouldered ... an ex-FBI agent ... with a reputation for taking the 'tough cases'"; Randall, "bow-tied," "craggy-faced," "Lincolnesque"; Segell, a "slender six-footer"; Victoria Miller, a "trim brunet beauty." A subsequent reference to a man was almost always by his last name, but a woman could be either "Mrs. Miller" or "Vicky." A woman's dress and shoe size—as well as her "vital statistics"—were de rigueur, at least when the woman was buxom, attractive, and on the sunny side of forty. (So were adjectives such as "buxom" and "attractive.") Thompson's every facial twitch, eye blink, and hand gesture seems to have been recorded. It is quite possible, for that matter, that no Twin Citian's wardrobe was ever known in greater detail by the newspaper-reading public than his.

Contrary to what occurred during the Sheppard case in Ohio, where public opinion ran heavily against the defendant and the local papers demanded his conviction, there was a general withholding of judgment, at least in the press coverage of Thompson's trial. Most Twin Citians probably believed that Thompson had arranged his wife's murder; still, there was no vilification of the defendant in the papers, nor any presumptive demands for a guilty verdict.

Only Thompson himself would insist that he had been a marked man from the beginning.

3.

The state of Minnesota built its case against Thompson on seven evidentiary "links," which Randall presented in his opening statement on November 4. Some of the alleged connections had been mentioned in the papers, while others, resulting from Barkley's ongoing investigation and the substantiation of informant accounts, were news to even close followers of the case. The six-man, six-woman jury, twenty-one to seventy-one years of age, including two housewives and mothers, listened intently as the prosecutor cited the "links" in turn.

- Thompson's removal of the telephone extension from the master bedroom two days prior to the murder.
- His removal of Schatzie, the family's dachshund—who, according to Randall, was known to bark excitedly at strangers—less than a month before the murder.
- The partially filled bathtub, the unlocked side door, and a rarely used security chain that had been fastened at the front door the morning of the murder.
- Thompson's atypically early appearance at his office the mornings of March 5 and 6.
- Thompson's payment of $2,500 cash (via a St. Paul attorney named John Connolly) to alleged middleman Norman Mastrian shortly after the murder.
- The $1.1 million worth of accidental-death policies on Carol Thompson, most of it purchased within a year of her murder.
- And Victoria Miller, a woman Randall said Thompson had dated, frequently slept with, and was determined to marry.

Any one or two of those links would be insufficient to convict, Randall told the jury, but together they formed a "solid chain" of circumstantial evidence that left no reasonable doubt that Thompson had planned and bankrolled Carol's murder.

Hy Segell, in his comparatively brief opening statement that followed the prosecutor's presentation, told the jury that the defense would establish that "Gene Thompson had no part in the commission of that offense, [and] that he was entirely incapable of committing such an offense by the very nature of his background, his profession, and his position in the community." Segell's strategy would be to provide a reasonable explanation for Randall's evidentiary connections. The defendant was planning, for instance, to replace the extension phone with a new Princess model that would better fit the home's updated décor, and Carol herself had agreed that their dog Schatzie's unreliable toilet habits posed a hazard to the new carpet, and the dog had to go to another home. The $2,500 that Thompson had directed to Mastrian was actually a returned "retainer" for legal work that had never been performed. Thompson, moreover, had confessed to his infidelity, Carol had forgiven him, and the affair with Vicky Miller had ended more than a year before the murder. As for the admittedly outsized insurance policies—well, those were the purchases of an impulsive and eccentric man who would not mind bragging to associates that he carried a million-plus dollars of coverage on his wife.

Between the end of jury selection on October 31 and the closing statements on December 5, a total of 107 witnesses would testify for prosecution and defense. These included the insurance agents who sold Thompson the controversial policies, the Northwestern Bell Telephone employee who had checked the jacks in the Thompson home following the murder, and Schatzie's new owner, who testified that the dog did indeed tend to bark when someone came to the door but did not seem to have a significant bladder-control problem. The "hoodlums" (Segell's term) Willard Ingram, Henry Butler, Richard Sharp, and Sheldon Morris testified for the state—Ingram, Butler, and Sharp each describing how he was offered, and rejected, the Thompson murder contract by Norman Mastrian before Mastrian struck a deal with Dick Anderson. Other state's witnesses included Otto Swoboda, Ruth Nelson, Dr. Fritz Pearson, Sergeant John Mercado, Drs. John Perry, Jr., and Kevin Lawler, Lieutenant George Barkley, Detective Ernest Williams, criminalist Theodore Elzerman, the burglarized Luger owner Wayne Brandt, Donald Kelly, and his and Thompson's secretary, Kathleen Zajacz. Several of the Thompsons' friends and neighbors, including Marjorie Young, the Robert Ericksons, Dr. and Mrs. Carl Koutsky, the Reverend William Paden, Yvonne Bengel, and Merlyn Erikson, as well as Thompson's sisters, Geraldine Gesche and Clarice Fager, his mother-in-law, Antonia Swoboda, and son, Jeff Thompson, took the stand for the defense. Mastrian, who continued to deny his involvement while remaining in police custody in St. Paul, was not called.

Yet only a few surprises emerged during the seemingly endless parade of diverse witnesses. Perhaps the ugliest, provided by Dick Anderson, was the revelation that Mastrian had mentioned several possible means of executing Carol Thompson—including a car bomb that would coincidentally kill a couple of her friends and thereby confuse police as to the actual target—and suggested that Otto Swoboda would be next on the Thompson hit list. More benign but almost as bizarre was the testimony of James Treanor, a friend and life-insurance broker, who said that in April 1962, eleven months before Carol's murder, Cotton told him he had had premonitions about the deaths of a sister and brother in traffic accidents years earlier and that he had been having similar visions involving Carol. Attempting to calm his overwrought friend—the two men had been lunching at the St. Paul Athletic Club—Treanor said he bet Cotton a malted milk that nothing terrible would happen to his wife.

Victoria Miller was the most eagerly anticipated witness, at least during the early part of the trial, dominated as it was by the testimony of insurance salesmen, telephone installers, and dog owners. Her appearance, on November 13, drew some of the trial's most titillating headlines. "Tearful 'Other Woman' Tells of Marriage Bid / Pert Beauty ... Testifies To Illicit Dates"—this from just the *Dispatch* on the afternoon of her testimony. " 'Other Woman' Bares Secrets of Her Romance With Thompson," the *Pioneer Press*'s unusually tabloidesque banner read the next morning.

First sobbing, then "almost chipper," according to the press reports, Vicky Miller described, at Randall's behest, a series of assignations with the defendant, in the Twin Cities and Forest Lake as well as during "business trips" to northern Minnesota and Illinois, over the course of about a year and a half, beginning in the summer of 1960. She said Thompson would often pay for a babysitter for her three small children (she was between marriages during most of their sexual relationship) and offered to pay her rent; for several months she worked as a stenographer in his office. One day, after they had broken up and she had married Michael Miller, she testified, Thompson said to her, "If I put $10,000 in the bank in your name, will you marry me?" She said she told him no.

But because the defense admitted the affair, and because Mrs. Miller confirmed that their sexual relations had ended in early 1962, after Thompson told her he would not leave his wife, her testimony could not have had much impact. The one statement that may have been important to the jury was the witness's description of a conversation she had with Thompson after he had supposedly confessed their affair to Carol in January or February 1962.

> He said, "Just give me a year," and I said, "No, after a year it will be two years and then three years," and I had to make something for myself, and he said, "Well, then just give me eleven months. I have done quite well in a year and I have my home practically paid for and I cannot expect Carol and my family to live on a lower level than they are used to living on right now. . . . If you will give me this time I feel that they would be well taken care of and then you and I could have enough money to live on also."

But, again, Mrs. Miller said, she did not bite.

By the end of the day, Randall had indubitably established that the avowed family man and church elder was also an avid adulterer who had thought about—had pleaded for—a life with a woman other than his wife. Segell, on cross-examination, had to settle for Vicky Miller's apparently genuine yet probably less convincing testimony that while Thompson had been unfaithful, he nonetheless respected his wife, never quarreled with her, and made it clear that, whatever he told Vicky on occasion, he would never leave her.

Afterward, at least one jury member said Mrs. Miller's testimony had not made any difference to the outcome.

4.

In the end, it would be the words of the two men who last saw Carol Thompson whole and unbloodied that almost certainly decided her husband's fate.

Bill Randall had worried about Dick Anderson's testimony. Anderson, after all, was a heavy-drinking drug abuser whose combat experience in Korea had possibly inflicted psychological damage as well as physical wounds. More to the point, Anderson was not, by any stretch of the imagination, a hardened "hit man"; he had more in common with the "stumblebums" (again, Hy Segell's term) Willard Ingram and Henry Butler than with a tough pug like Norman Mastrian. While that might have made Anderson more talkative in a police interrogation room, it might also make him less predictable, more skittish, on the witness stand—an ill-equipped match for a seasoned litigator such as Segell. Randall believed that Anderson was a "weak character," not the kind of witness on whom a prosecutor would choose to base his case. To make matters worse, Anderson would take the stand when court resumed on November 26, the day after John Kennedy's funeral. Who knew what anybody's mood and attention span would be in the wash of the staggering national trauma?

Randall need not have fretted. Anderson effectively and in excruciating detail described the horrific assault on Carol Thompson, and convincingly linked, through Mastrian, T. Eugene Thompson to Carol's death.

In the *Dispatch*, staff writers J. C. Wolfe and Max Swartz portrayed the prosecution's star witness as somberly dressed, in a dark gray suit, white shirt, and dark tie, "appearing somewhat nervous and at times hesitant in his narrative." In the next morning's *Pioneer Press*, Giese described a "handsome man with dark brown hair, prominent brows, and a square jaw" telling "in precise, carefully chosen words and a calm, even tone a chilling tale of cold-blooded murder." So matter-of-fact was Anderson's account, Giese added, that the killer "might have been discussing some of the building materials he once sold rather than the gruesome bludgeoning and stabbing of Carol Thompson."

The typewritten pages of the trial transcript, with their numbered lines and metronomic Q and *A*, have none of the visual or verbal enhancements of the newspaper reports. But the stark language of Anderson's testimony is all the more powerful thus uncolored—and is unrelenting even under Segell's vigorous cross-examination.

Early in his direct questioning, Randall asked the witness about his rendezvous with Mastrian on the evening of March 4.

Q: After you got in [Mastrian's car], what occurred?

A: We discussed the contract further.

Q: Do you recall what was said?

A: He says, "Well, I could only come up with $200," but he said, "I will be able to pay you the rest on this coming Friday." And then there was other general conversation and he says, "One of the two—it will have to look like an accident. . . . The broad's father will be next in six or seven months." And then he went into detail on how this was supposed to be set up.

Q: What did he say as to how it was supposed to be set up?

A: This was the first time I had heard the name of Mr. Thompson. He says, "Mr. Thompson will leave the door open in the morning." He says, "You'll be able to go inside and go down the basement and wait." He says, "At 8:25 Mr. Thompson will call Mrs. Thompson," and he says, "At that time you will be able to sneak up the stairway." He says, "Mrs. Thompson will be right around in the kitchen answering the telephone. The other telephones in the house will be removed so that she has to come downstairs."

Anderson then told of driving with Mastrian to Highland Park, where they cruised past 1720 Hillcrest several times before parking in front of the house. (The street was dark by early evening.) Mastrian, Anderson said, pointed out the side door and assured him that no one would be out and about that early in the morning. "You won't have to worry about anybody seeing you," he said Mastrian told him.

"I then also discussed with [Mastrian] the price and said, '$2,000 is not enough money.' He says, 'If you succeed in making this look like an accident, I'll pay you $4,000.' I said, 'Better than that, I'll take $3,000, whether it is an accident or not,' and we agreed on those terms—$3,000."

Anderson said Mastrian then produced the rubber "whopper" from under the car's front seat and instructed him on the angle at which he should strike the back of the woman's head—"to more or less simulate falling in the bathtub"—and how he should then place her, unconscious and on her back, in the tub. Mr. Thompson, he said Mastrian told him, would leave the tub filled with water.

Anderson said that when he asked Mastrian why the woman was going to be murdered, Mastrian replied, "Well, she must have done something terrible because he must hate her to do this." To which Anderson said, "Mastrian, I don't believe you, because it must be insurance or something if you want it to look like an accident." Mastrian, he said, then conceded that insurance was involved. Anderson was apparently satisfied with Mastrian's explanation, because he said the two men, without further discussion of Thompson's motives, drove to a coffee shop nearby where Mastrian diagrammed the house's layout on a paper napkin.

Randall asked about the door locks, including the "chain latch" on the front door that Anderson said Mastrian promised would be fastened, presumably so no one could walk in on the killer before he was done. Then the prosecutor inquired about the dog. Anderson said Mastrian, while they were scouting the neighborhood, told him the family dog had already been removed.

> Q: Was there anything further said when you made the second trip up around the house?
>
> A: Yes, sir, there was. I said, "What happens if Mr. Thompson or somebody else comes downstairs while I am down there in the morning?" and he said, "You don't have to worry about that because I told Mr. Thompson I would kill him if he came down in the basement." He said, "He thinks I am doing the job."

Then Randall guided Anderson through the murder itself. The killer recounted turning off his alarm early on the morning of March 5 and deciding, "I wasn't going to do the job"; his acquisition of the stolen Luger from Mastrian later that day; and his jittery preparations the morning of March 6: "I got up, put on my slippers, and went directly to the refrigerator and mixed a double [shot of vodka]. I drank that, had another one, and I went in and shaved, washed up, put on a suit, white shirt, tie, got out an old overcoat[,] . . . had another drink, put on the coat, and went downstairs and went to the rear of the car—got out the rubber hose, also picked up the gun before I left the apartment, went downstairs and got the hat and coat out of the rear of the car, put them on the front seat beside me, got in the car, went up the Mall, turned right on Hennepin. . . ." He told about parking the car a block and a half from the Thompsons' home, walking in the snow along the dark, all-but-deserted streets to 1720 Hillcrest (he said he spotted a newsboy making his rounds, but the boy apparently did not see him), entering the house through the side door, and waiting in the basement for two hours and twenty minutes. From his hiding place, he said, he heard snippets of conversation from the main floor, including Mr. Thompson telling someone that he did not have time for coffee. Every few minutes, he would check the time on his wristwatch, using a pen light he carried in his pocket. When, at about a quarter after eight, Mr. Thompson and the children were finally gone, and having revised his plan on account of the squeaky basement steps, he said he waited for his victim to answer the phone call from her husband and return to bed. Then he crept upstairs.

From the deserted first floor, he quietly proceeded to the second.

Q: Where was [Mrs. Thompson] at this time?

A: She was sitting up in bed. She had the light on right next to her, the radio was on, and she was reading a magazine with her glasses on when she looked at me.

Anderson, who had replaced his winter gloves with surgical gloves and now brandished the Luger, said he told her, "Turn your head so you don't see me." Assuring her that he was only after money, he told her to take off her glasses and lie on her stomach with her face away from him. Then: "I took out the whopper, or hose, whatever you want to call it, with both hands and put it crossways on her skull and reached up and hit her as hard as I could."

Anderson testified that he removed the unconscious woman's nightgown and carried her down the hall to the bathroom, where the tub was filled with several inches of water. Following Mastrian's instructions, he lowered the woman into the water and began pressing on her chest—the "reverse artificial respiration" that was supposed to simulate a drowning.

Q: What then, if anything, happened?

A: She came to.

Q: What then happened?

A: With [the] surgical gloves and the wet water and everything, she slipped out of my grasp somehow. She managed to get out of the tub.

While Anderson struggled to retrieve the pistol from his overcoat pocket, Mrs. Thompson ran out of the bathroom and down the hallway to her bedroom.

Q: As you went into the master bedroom, was Mrs. Thompson there?

A: She was, sir.

Q: What then occurred?

A: She was putting on her bathrobe.

Q: As she put on her bathrobe, what if anything did you do?

A: I had the gun pointed at her, I was right close to her, and at this time she said, "Don't do this. My husband is a criminal lawyer. He'll protect you from the police."

Q: Did you say anything?

A: No, sir.

Q: What did you do?

A: I pulled the trigger.

Q: At the time you pulled the trigger what, if anything, occurred to the gun?

A: Nothing.

Q: What occurred as far as Mrs. Thompson was concerned?

A: At this point things started moving rather fast. I remember I dropped the pillow [that he had wrapped around the pistol as a makeshift silencer], hit the gun with my left hand.

Q: What did she do at that point?

A: Well, she started to come my way and tried to get past me. . . .

Q: Did you have contact with her at that point? Was there a physical meeting between you?

A: I believe that's when I hit her the first time, sir.

Q: What did you hit her with?

A: The butt of the pistol.

Q: What did she do?

A: I believe she fell at this point and got back up again and when I was ejecting the shell out of the chamber and put another shell into the Luger, while I was doing that she got past me and ran down the hallway and down the stairway.

Q: What did you do?

A: I followed her.

Q: How close behind were you?

A: Not very far.

Q: When she got to the bottom of the stairs, what did she do?

A: She went to the front door, sir. . . .

Q: What occurred at the front door?

A: She managed to get the door open as far as the chain lock would let the door open.

Q: At that point what then occurred?

A: She screamed. I got the door closed and pulled her away from it.

Q: After you had pulled her away from the door, what occurred?

A: I commenced hitting her.

Q: With what were you hitting her?

A: With the butt of the Luger.

Q: You hit her more than once?

A: Yes, sir.

Q: After you struck her with the Luger, what did she do?

A: She took off her diamond ring. She says, "Here, take this."

Q: Did you take it from her?

A: Yes, sir.

Q: What happened at the time you took it from her?

A: I think I dropped it on the floor there.

Q: After dropping the diamond ring, what did you do?

A: I hit her again.

Q: Was she standing at this time?

A: She was in a kneeling position.

Q: After striking her again, what did you do?

A: She said, "Oh God, help me."

Anderson's direct testimony—occasionally interrupted by the defense's objections, most of which were overruled—continued. With more of the same kind of detail dispassionately, even courteously rendered, the killer recounted stabbing Carol Thompson repeatedly with the paring knife he found in the kitchen, leaving her for dead, and moments later—while he hurriedly washed his hands and face in the second-floor bathroom and then, in the bedroom, attempted to make the assault look as though it had been part of a burglary—her improbable escape out the side door. Nearly as unlikely was his own departure and block-and-a-half walk, now in broad daylight, to his parked car, apparently unnoticed by anyone along the way.

The remaining detail was superfluous. It would be hard to believe that anyone in the room—surely not the members of the jury—had ever heard anything like Anderson's narrative, nor needed to hear more to be convinced of the horror of both the jerry-built setup and its bungled execution.

As it happened, the most explosive reaction—near the climax of Anderson's direct testimony—was that of the defendant himself. Don Giese, who was sitting only a few feet away, wrote:

> [Thompson's] hands and arms were trembling violently. His face cracked into agitated contortions. Tears were streaming down his face. And when Anderson calmly said his victim had pleaded, "Oh, God help me," Thompson lifted himself halfway out of his chair and, in a sob-wracked voice, shouted to Anderson, "Oh, God help you!" He fell forward on the counsel table and wept. Judge Fosseen declared a recess and Thompson was escorted from the room by his lawyers.

Contrary to expectations, Anderson, for his part, retained his composure under Segell's aggressive cross. He stuck to the details of his story while calmly denying that he had learned those details from the newspapers or been instructed by the police. Typical was the following exchange initiated by Segell, who asked if the witness had met Mastrian for the first time on March 3. Anderson had said yes.

Q: Is it your habit to take up contract killing with strangers?
A: No, sir.
Q: Is it your habit to take up contract killing for $200 down?
A: It is not my habit to take up contract killing at all.

Anderson denied that he was in the house to steal money, or for any other purpose than to murder Carol Thompson.

Segell excused the witness, and, shortly afterward, the prosecution rested its case.

5.

Three days after his outburst, and following the soothing words of friendly witnesses testifying to the felicity of his marriage, T. Eugene Thompson took the stand in his own defense. Dressed for the occasion in a dark blue suit and the customary matching accessories, he seemed to be his more familiarly controlled and confident self. As he sat down in the witness box, Giese noted, a "slight smile stole across his boyish face."

In more than eleven hours of direct testimony and cross-examination over the course of three days, Thompson declaimed at length—often in far greater detail than was requested or required—on his background, education, courtship of Carol, marriage, professional career, business interests, financial dealings, personal relationships, and activities in the days and weeks surrounding March 6. As for the seven "links" that supposedly connected him to the murder, he had an explanation for each of them. On the key points of contention, he testified, in no uncertain terms, that he loved his wife and children, that he had confessed to and been forgiven for his adultery, and that he had purchased the million-plus dollars of life insurance in the name of long-term financial security for his family.

"Did you hire anybody to kill your wife?" Segell asked at the end of his direct.

"No. I did not," Thompson replied.

"Did you do anything whatsoever to effect the death of your wife, Carol Thompson?"

"I did not."

People who knew him could not have been surprised that Thompson, as headstrong and self-assured as he was, chose to testify, though it is highly doubtful that his counsel would have been pleased with either the testimony or its delivery. (Neither Segell nor Fallon ever publicly commented on the matter.) Compared with Anderson's polite, direct, and unemotional answers, the lion's share of the defendant's responses were, by almost any standard, variously supercilious, condescending, bombastic, incomplete, incomprehensible, and unconvincing.

When Segell asked him about his "insurance consciousness," for example, Thompson responded:

> Well, I feel this way . . . there are certain things in life you can control and certain things you cannot control. Now, if you can afford to guarantee in the nature of replacement value—what I am talking about now, and things like this—property insurance—well, then it's foolish not to. The same way, you should be responsible for your own acts. Therefore, if you drive an automobile, you should fully insure it so that if you cause damage to someone else, you should be there to be responsible for that damage.

On the subject of adultery, Thompson recalled his mea culpa—and Carol's reaction—this way:

> Actually it was a very short conversation. I started to tell her about it. I said, "Hon, I got something I want to say, get off my chest," and I said, "I have been doing a little bit of running around for quite a while." She said, "That's enough. I know who it was. I knew all about it. I was quite certain you would come to your own good sense and would handle it in your own way." That was the last we discussed it.

Regarding his reaction to Sidney Nelson's phone call on the morning of March 6, Thompson explained why he had driven from his downtown office to Hillcrest Avenue instead of going directly to the hospital:

> Well, the difference in time is not very great and I wanted to make sure that I got there. He said that she had been hurt.

Both his tone and his demeanor changed dramatically when Randall began his cross-examination. Rolling his eyes, sighing impatiently, often beginning his answers before Randall had completed the question, Thompson came across as unabashedly contemptuous of the plodding, unflappable prosecutor, whom he sometimes addressed, with patronizing familiarity, as "Bill."

One exchange between the two—regarding a meeting Thompson had arranged, a few weeks after Carol's murder, with Mastrian, who had not yet been arrested—went as follows:

Q: What was the occasion for meeting him in [lawyer John] Connolly's office on Good Friday?

A: I wanted him to help me trace that gun [the pistol whose broken grip had been recovered at the crime scene].

Q: Would you care to advise the court and jury why you thought he [Mastrian] would be able to trace that gun?

A: He had lived in Minneapolis all his life. He is well acquainted in Minneapolis. In 1952 he was convicted of burglary. I just had the feeling that he could help me if he tried, like going around to the bars and doing things I could not do personally.

Q: What was the occasion for deciding that this was something that should be done in the bars in Minneapolis?

A: I also had hopes of going around St. Paul.

Q: Did you have hopes that someone would help you in St. Paul or did you plan to do that yourself?

A: I am not totally unfamiliar with the bars in St. Paul.

And yet another, on the subject of the defendant's infidelity:

A: During my marriage I went out with one woman [Vicky]. I will make that as a flat statement, Mr. Randall, I'll state that flatly, so there will be no doubt in yours or anyone's mind. Don't be so foolish as to ask me if I ever took any [other women] out to lunch or anything. I am talking about dating for the purposes of other things.

Q: Why would that be so foolish?

A: Because I would have to answer you that I have gone out many, many times.

6.

Thompson's testimony ended, without fireworks or epiphany, on December 3. The defense then introduced a handful of family members to reinforce the idea that Cotton, while admittedly "impulsive," had been a wonderful husband and father who was "devastated" by Carol's death. The Thompsons' marriage, said one of these latter witnesses, Cotton's sister Geraldine, had "seemed like ... an extended honeymoon."

The final witness for the defense, on the afternoon of December 3, was Jeffrey Thompson, now fourteen and a half years old, the oldest of the Thompson children. Segell had two apparent reasons for calling the boy to the stand. First, his presence would reinforce the defendant's image as a family man. Meticulously dressed in the green and khaki uniform required of St. Paul Academy cadets, Jeff was swaddled in the baby fat of early adolescence. Still, with his horn-rimmed glasses and thatch of blond hair, he bore an almost comical resemblance to the short, bespectacled, fair-haired man seated a few feet in front of him. No one in the room would have had the slightest doubt whose son he was.

Jeff's testimony, moreover, would be an additional attempt to create or reinvigorate whatever doubt the jurors might have had about Dick Anderson's credibility. A week earlier Anderson had testified that the basement in the Thompson home was dark during the nearly two and a half hours he waited there. Now, under oath, Jeff was asked if there had been a light burning in the basement that morning.

"Yes, there was," Jeff replied, adding, after Segell's follow-up, that, at his mother's request, he had gone downstairs and turned it off.

Jeff further testified, following Segell's questions, that he recalled his father coming down to the dining room for breakfast on March 6 and that—contrary to Anderson's testimony—his father never said he did not have time for coffee.

During Randall's equally brief and gentle cross, the boy told the court that his father had first asked him about the basement light during a drive down to Elmore in August. Jeff also said he had told his uncle Wally—Wallace Thompson, his father's brother, an attorney with a private practice in southern Minnesota—about the basement light, this during the family's Thanksgiving gathering in November.

Jeff's responses to Randall's queries, as they had been to Segell's, were businesslike and succinct, in marked contrast to his father's.

Q: Where was the light, please?

A: It was in the rec room. . . .

Q: And where is the switch?

A: It is in the hall . . . at the base of the stairs.

Q: When you turned to go down from the kitchen, did you notice whether the light was on?

A: Yes.

Q: You could see it from up on the kitchen-floor level?

A: Yes.

Neither Randall nor Segell had further questions, and the boy was excused.

Later that afternoon, after the court had been adjourned for the day, T. Eugene Thompson hugged his son and shook his hand. He said he was pleased with Jeff's testimony. Then he presented the boy with a grown-up wristwatch—a manly, gold-plated Hamilton with a square face, Roman numerals, and the initials *T.E.T.* engraved on the case.

7.

On Thursday, December 5, the prosecution and defense presented their final arguments.

Randall reiterated, over the course of two hours, the extensive, albeit circumstantial, evidence against T. Eugene Thompson, enumerating for the jurors, one more time, the "seven links" that he said proved Thompson had hired Norman Mastrian to effect the murder of his wife, making Thompson as guilty of first-degree murder as the actual killer, Dick Anderson. Randall reminded the jury that circumstantial evidence was as valid as direct ("No one had to tell Robinson Crusoe that he saw a man on the island. He himself saw a footprint in the sand"), and ridiculed the defendant's "happy honeymooner" image. At any rate, he said, "There is no known measuring stick with which you can look at a man and determine from his appearance, even from his past conduct, whether he did or did not do a given act on a given day."

Segell likewise took about two hours to conclude the defense's case. He once more attacked the state's "links," comparing them to "a pile of paper clips that, [when] dropped to the floor, scatter and are nothing." On the matter of the insurance, for instance, he acknowledged that his client "may be a little eccentric, he may be a little egocentric. Maybe he enjoyed telling his friends, 'I just bought another quarter million on Carol.' But this isn't the issue in this case, whether I have an impulsive, egocentric client. The issue is whether he hired someone to kill his wife." Segell dismissed the testimony of the "hoodlums" who had taken the stand for the prosecution, suggesting deals cut with the county attorney and an attempt to shift the blame for what really happened on March 6—most probably, an interrupted burglary that spiraled into murder.

In the absence of "one word that would indicate malice or hatred by Gene Thompson for his wife," Segell concluded, "you have to believe that this man was a monster. You have to believe that he planned his wife's murder knowing that his children would come home to lunch and find this woman either drowned in a bathtub, stabbed and beaten, lying in a pool of blood or blown up with dynamite. He has to be that kind of a monster in your mind before you can find this man guilty of this offense."

Judge Fosseen gave the jury their instructions—there could be one of only two possible verdicts: guilty or not guilty of first-degree murder—and, at 4:00 PM, December 5, the panel began their ultimate obligation.

The other principals could do nothing but wait. Whatever their expectations, neither side of the counsels' table said anything publicly at the time—though much later both sides expressed doubts about their respective chances. "It was hard to see the forest for the trees," Fallon recalled. "I thought we had a good, fighting chance, though they had a strong circumstantial case. You can read Thompson's testimony. His case was, 'I don't know anything about this. I didn't hire Norman Mastrian. I didn't want my wife killed.' That was our defense. He broke down and cried during Anderson's testimony. You wouldn't think a guilty man would react that way." Randall said, "I felt the odds were three to one against conviction. Thompson had a good background and reputation, and he said he didn't do it. All we had were a bunch of crumbums testifying against him—not the sort of stellar witnesses the jury could identify with. I didn't sleep the night before the verdict. I knew he was guilty, but I was apprehensive."

The defendant, for his part, sat down with a pair of local television reporters for a twenty-five minute interview arranged by Bill Fallon. Elegantly dressed as always, speaking in a soft, flat, slightly nasal voice, smoking cigarettes and once in a while showing the slightest trace of a smile, T. Eugene was obviously tired, yet seemed relaxed and composed. Patiently answering the interviewers' questions, he reminisced about his boyhood in Elmore, explained the satisfactions of a law career, and recounted the love and pride he felt for his children, who had done "remarkably well" during the family's ordeal. Though he was not asked what he thought the verdict would be, he tried to sound optimistic. "I truly believe justice will be done," he said.

Shortly after six o'clock on the following evening, December 6,

after twelve hours and twenty minutes of deliberation, the jury returned their verdict: Tilmer Eugene Thompson was guilty as
charged.

Exactly nine months after Carol Thompson's murder, Judge
Fosseen, at the prosecution's request, sentenced her husband—
now ashen-faced, silent, and fighting back tears—to life in prison,
beginning the next day.

8.

News of the Thompson verdict made headlines from New York to
Honolulu and beyond. Newspapers in Norway and Australia carried wire-service accounts of the trial's outcome. A college friend
of Bill Randall who had become the U.S. ambassador to Ethiopia
sent congratulations from Addis Ababa.

In the Twin Cities, the Thompson saga again dominated the
front pages of the daily papers and topped local newscasts. While
not everybody agreed with the verdict, no one outside of T. Eugene's family circle seemed especially surprised, much less outraged or even disappointed by it. After nine months, the prevailing
emotion among the public was most likely relief.

Among Thompson's family and friends, the responses were
more complicated. During a family dinner the night before, Douglas Young had advised T. Eugene's sisters and brother to be "prepared for the very worst." Nonetheless, when the verdict arrived,
the defendant's siblings were stunned and heartbroken. "My little
family and I are spending the night praying to God for strength to
accept what has happened," Clarice Fager told a reporter. "And
praying that some time in the future my brother's innocence will
be proven."

Contacted moments after the verdict was announced, Otto Swoboda, at home with his wife, declined to comment.

Neither Norman Mastrian nor Dick Anderson, according to their jailers, said anything memorable upon hearing the news.

Vicky Miller told the *Pioneer Press*, "That family is in enough distress without me opening my mouth anymore."

For his part, the ubiquitous Doug Young—he had picked up Jeff Thompson at school the day Carol was attacked, distributed T. Eugene's "explanatory statement" on March 26, and been present when Thompson was arrested on June 21—was now, on the evening of December 6, responsible for telling the Thompson children that their father had been found guilty of their mother's murder and would not be coming home.

"They took it very well," Young told the *Dispatch* the next day. "We all had tears."

Carol and Cotton Thompson stride into married life, March 27, 1948. Years later, Thompson told his son, "We don't believe in divorce in this family." (Courtesy Margaret Wilson)

Jeff, Patty, left, and Margaret, circa 1957. (Courtesy Margaret Wilson)

Wearing dresses made by their mother, Margaret, Amy, and Patty pose with Jeff and Carol in a formal portrait about two years before Carol's murder. (Courtesy Margaret Wilson)

Blood-stained footprints mark the killer's escape from the Thompson home on the morning of March 6, 1963. Police covered some of the footprints with cardboard, circled, to protect them from the falling snow. (Don Spavin, St. Paul Dispatch)

Detectives began gathering in front of 1720 Hillcrest—"the scene of a cutting"—within an hour of the attack on Carol Thompson. (St. Paul Dispatch)

T. Eugene Thompson, wearing a hat, arrives for arraignment in municipal court hours after his arrest on June 21, 1963. As always, the "prominent attorney" was impeccably attired—minus the usual necktie, which had been removed by police at his booking. His escort included homicide commander George Barkley, right. (T. J. Strasser, St. Paul Dispatch)

Defense attorney Hyam Segell, left, shares a cigarette break with prosecutor William Randall during Thompson's trial. Thompson's lawyers felt they had a "fighting chance" of drawing a not-guilty verdict; Randall believed the odds were "three to one against conviction." (Sylvan Doroshow, St. Paul Dispatch)

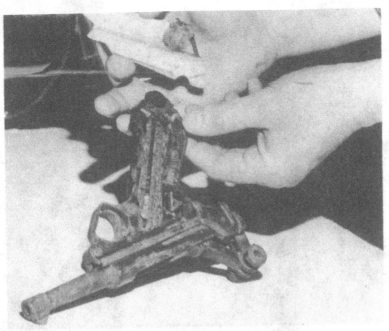

Retrieved from a marsh almost two months after the murder, the killer's rusted Luger bears the effects—including missing handle grips and bent trigger guard—of the brutal assault. (Hi Paul, St. Paul Dispatch)

"Middleman" Norman Mastrian at the beginning of his trial, in Duluth, in February 1964. Eight weeks later, he was convicted of first-degree murder. (St. Paul Pioneer Press)

Convicted of first-degree murder, Thompson awaits processing behind bars at the Stillwater state prison on December 7, 1963, almost exactly nine months after his wife's murder. (St. Paul Pioneer Press)

Dick Anderson leaves court after his testimony. Despite prosecutors' fears, Anderson was convincing and unshakable in his sworn account of both the bizarre murder plot and its bungled execution. (Sylvan Doroshow, St. Paul Dispatch)

Carol's parents, Antonia and Otto Swoboda, leave a probate court hearing on January 7, 1964. Following a bitter struggle with T. Eugene's siblings, the Swobodas were granted custody of the Thompson children and kept the siblings together in Highland Park through their high school years. (Hi Paul, St. Paul Dispatch)

Judge Jeffrey Thompson of Minnesota's Third Judicial District, in Winona, September 2005. (Mark Miranda, courtesy Jeffrey Thompson)

PART TWO

Brother and Sisters

[Daddy] said: "All children must look after their own upbringing." Parents can only give good advice or put them on the right paths, but the final forming of a person's character lies in their own hands.

- ANNE FRANK
  The Diary of a Young Girl

Murderer's Mark

1.

The day their mother died had begun ordinarily enough, though, several months later, at their father's trial, there would be significant disagreement about some of the details, which, in retrospect, would not seem ordinary at all.

Decades later, Jeff Thompson remembered his mother calling him from the hallway on the second floor, waking him from a deep sleep in his third-floor bedroom. It was seven o'clock on a Wednesday morning, a school day like any other. It was just getting light, and the wooden floor was cold where there was not a rug, and when Jeff looked past his reflection in the window, he could see that it was snowing. Slowly, reluctantly, the way a thirteen-year-old boy ambulates on a cold, dark school-day morning, he descended the stairs to the bathroom on the second floor, washed his face, and dressed for the day in St. Paul Academy's winter uniform: a green-and-khaki ensemble with a black necktie, Sam Browne belt, and spit-shined oxfords. Jeff was short for his age and chubby. He wore thick glasses and a military-style crew cut like his father's.

Breakfast that morning was bacon and eggs. Jeff remembered eating at the dining-room table, which would later be one point of contention. (His father testified that the family had breakfasted that morning in the kitchen.) He would also recall his father's presence at the table, which no one disputed, but which Jeff and his sisters would later agree was out of the ordinary. His father was usually still in bed when Jeff and his sisters left for school. A few weeks earlier, his father, having decided that Jeff needed to lose weight, decreed that the boy get up at six-thirty every weekday morning for a vigorous session of Navy calisthenics. The first morning his father led the exercises. The second morning Jeff did them by himself. After that, the workouts were not mentioned again. In any case, that had been an anomaly in the Thompson household. "We never saw him in the morning," Jeff said later.

Also unusual, according to Jeff, were his father's offer of a ride to school (Jeff almost always walked) and his father's directive to latch the safety chain on the front door before they departed, as usual, by the door at the side of the house. It was shortly after eight o'clock when he and his father left the house that day. Outside, the temperature was at the freezing mark and the light snow Jeff had seen from his bedroom window continued to fall. It was not a long drive—s.p.a. was only a couple of minutes away—and Jeff would not recall what, if anything, he and his father talked about en route. "Generally, we didn't talk much to each other," Jeff said years later. "Though I remember being talked *to* a lot."

Once at school, Jeff fell into his Wednesday morning routine. He was in second form, or eighth grade, at s.p.a., which he later described as "a posh scholastic prison for boys with wealthy parents." Dissatisfied with his lackadaisical study habits and mediocre grades, his parents had transferred him there from the public middle school in Highland Park at the beginning of the academic year. He was a bright but unambitious boy whose consuming passion, to his parents' chagrin, was his cache of more than five hundred comic books detailing the adventures of Superman, Spiderman, Flash, the Green Lantern, and other fantastic heroes. He had struggled during his first half year at S.P.A., particularly in an accelerated math class for which his previous school had inadequately prepared him. Now, in the year's second semester, he had been placed in a somewhat less rigorous class—"dumbbell math," the kids inevitably, if unfairly, called it—and he was doing much better.

He was in that class, sometime after ten o'clock on the morning of March 6, when he was summoned to the headmaster's office. "I was not a discipline problem, so [the call] was a mystery," he said later. In the office he was surprised to see his great-aunt Helen Zabel and his father's friend Douglas Young. They told him that his mother was in the hospital. They said she had been attacked by a man and was badly hurt. Then, providing little additional information, they drove him to the Zabels' house on Rome Avenue, a few blocks from home.

Recalling that morning's events—suddenly out of the ordinary, suddenly unlike anything he had experienced or even imagined in his thirteen years—Jeff would vividly remember a few of the sights and sounds that surrounded him, but not much else. His sisters—Patricia, Margaret, and Amy, retrieved at or on the way home from school—were already at the Zabels' house when he arrived.

"We had lunch and watched from the hallway as the adults . . . watched the news on Aunt Helen's TV," Jeff wrote later. The children were not supposed to see what they saw, but, probably because the adults themselves had been blindsided by something extraordinary, the latter let their guard down, and there, on the midday news, Jeff saw policemen walking in and out of his house, 1720 Hillcrest Avenue, and, a moment later, a person covered in a white sheet, whom he understood to be his mother, being rushed down a hallway on a cart while a man in a white coat, obviously a doctor, jogged alongside, leaning over her, pushing up and down on her chest.

After lunch at the Zabels', Jeff, apparently with permission from his elders, walked back to S.P.A. (Patricia likewise returned to school.) He would not remember what he had felt or was thinking as he scuffled along the snowy sidewalks by himself. He did recall that when he was back at the academy he told the kids standing next to him in choir class that his mother had been attacked—stabbed by a strange man. Then, for the second time that day, he was called down to the headmaster's office. This time he was greeted by Marjorie Young, Doug Young's wife and one of his mother's best friends, and the Reverend William Paden, the family's pastor, from Edgcumbe Presbyterian Church. Paden told Jeff that his mother was dead. Jeff retrieved his overcoat and rode back with the somber adults to the Zabels' home in Highland Park.

The house was crowded. It was filling with friends and relatives, including aunts, uncles, and cousins from out of town. There were several adults whom Jeff had never seen—people from his father's law office downtown and a couple of large men in overcoats who he was told were detectives. His St. Paul grandparents—Otto and Antonia Swoboda—had arrived from the hospital, and not far behind them came his dad, accompanied by more relatives and friends and people Jeff did not know. Nearly everybody except the detectives, Jeff would recall, was crying.

2.

This was a day that would change their lives, yet, decades later, there was so much that Jeff and his sisters could not remember, or remembered imperfectly. They would recall odd, seemingly unconnected details, but forget large blocks of time, important individuals, and major events, or realize that they did not know—maybe never knew—those things in the first place.

In an unfinished manuscript he began in 1986, twenty-three years after his mother's murder, Jeff recalled his father, recently arrived at Helen Zabel's house on the afternoon of March 6, walking into his cousin Ricky's bedroom off the dining room on the first floor and sobbing uncontrollably. The four Thompson children, assembled from various parts of the house, were ushered into Ricky's room to join their father. "T. Eugene was crying, rubbing his eyes with his hands, glasses off his face and held by the bow with one hand," Jeff wrote. Seeing their father distraught, the children started to cry. "T. Eugene professed his love for us and for Carol," Jeff continued, "and, after a time, we left him alone."

The oldest of Jeff's sisters, Patricia, would later recall the scene at the Zabels' house somewhat differently. "That morning I remember walking in, and Jeff was sitting in a chair staring at the television, and there were a whole bunch of grown-ups around—Grandma and Grandpa, Helen and Harry [Zabel], my aunts on my father's side, I think—and they were all talking in hushed tones," she said. "We kids were kind of shushed off into another room and kept away from the others. They just said that Mom was hurt. Then I went back to school. Then Helen came and took me out of school again because Mom had died. We went back to Helen's house, and Dad came in and hugged me so hard I thought *I* was going to die."

Patricia recalled that she had had a disturbing dream not long before her mother died. "I dreamt that she had dropped me off at the corner—at the Nelsons' house, which in the dream was a grocery store—where I was supposed to wait. I waited and waited, for hours and hours, and finally Dad came and said Mom wasn't coming back. I woke up in a cold sweat and went in and looked at Mom and went back to bed. On the day my mom died and we were pulled out of school and taken to Aunt Helen's house, I remembered that dream."

Amy, who was only six when her mother died, retained a precise, if problematic, recollection of the day. "I remember coming home from school for lunch," she said almost forty years later, "and the back [side] door was locked. I thought that was odd because the back door was never locked, and then I thought I would crawl through the little door where the milkman stuck the milk in the morning. I had my head in that little door when my great-aunt Helen drove up and called my name. She was terribly upset." Amy did not remember seeing police officers, or any other adults, in the yard that late morning, nor was it apparent why she had not been picked up at school as her siblings had.

"Helen didn't say anything in the car about my mother," she recalled. "She drove me back to her house, and my brother and sisters were already there, and I asked if she could make me macaroni and cheese. Typical kid. It had to be Kraft. [Later] we were at her house watching TV and saw, you know, like a news break. That's my memory of it anyway. I remember them saying the name on TV, 'Carol Thompson,' and I thought, 'That's my mom's name.' They showed a table with a sheet over a body, and for some reason I knew what that meant—that somebody was dead. I didn't realize it was my mom. Everyone else, I'm sure, realized she was dead before I did."

Only Jeff would recall talking to the police officers in his cousin's bedroom that afternoon. He remembered sitting at his cousin Ricky's desk, surrounded by "several big men—huge guys," though police records indicate that only two detectives,

Grant Willinger and Fred Buechner, asked questions. With their notebooks and serious expressions, they reminded Jeff of Joe Friday and Frank Smith on *Dragnet,* one of his favorite TV shows. He would recall their asking if he had seen anything unusual around the house that morning, or any strangers in the neighborhood—though, again, police files suggest that most if not all of the questions Willinger and Buechner asked involved such rather more mundane subjects as the unlocked side door. Jeff remembered his father saying, "You just tell them the truth." "But I doubt if we gave them any clues of value," Jeff wrote later. "We didn't have any."

The adults watched the evening news, which headlined the assault and murder of a prominent lawyer's wife in fashionable Highland Park, and tried to keep the children busy with other things. Steve Gesche, a seventeen-year-old cousin from Blue Earth, took Jeff for a ride down Ford Parkway and around Highland Village, the shopping area of Highland Park. Steve told Jeff that there must be some kind of lunatic running around out there in the darkness because only a crazy man could have done such a horrible thing to Jeff's mom.

That night the three girls were put to bed in a large upstairs room at the Zabels' house. Jeff went home with the Swobodas, where he would sleep in the familiar double bed in the upstairs room that Grandpa Otto used as a home office and where Jeff had spent the night on happier occasions in the past.

At the Zabels', Amy lay in bed and spoke to her mother. Decades later she recalled the conversation. "I said something like, 'How can I live without you?' And my mother said, 'If you dream of me, I'll be there. If you don't dream of me, it's because you don't need me.' It was her voice. It was not a dream. Patty and Maggie were sleeping, but I was awake. I felt better. Her voice calmed me. And then I was able to sleep."

A mile away, at his grandparents' house, Jeff lay on his back and stared at the ceiling. After a long, strange day that had begun like most other days, then had suddenly and inexplicably filled with weeping relatives and family friends, and then with detectives who wrote in their notebooks what he and his sisters said to them, he was finally alone. He had run out of tears, at least for the time being. Staring into the dark, he felt as though he were watching another boy's life in a movie. He knew, though, that the boy in the movie was him.

He replayed the events of that morning, then, despite himself, thought about the terrible scene from the previous afternoon. On Tuesday, he had come home from school and climbed the stairs to his bedroom on the third floor. It was his weekday routine. Returning home after school, he would go upstairs, change out of his uniform, and sit down with a snack and his hundreds of superhero comic books, arranging and rearranging them in neat stacks and pulling out one or two of his favorites to read. On that Tuesday afternoon, however, he was stunned to discover that his comic books were gone. The little attic hideout off his bedroom where he kept his stash had been emptied. He clambered downstairs and told his mother, who briskly informed him that she and his father had determined that he was spending too much time with his comic books and as a result they had decided to destroy them. She said that while he was at school that day she had burned the comics in the trash. Furious, Jeff screamed at her, "I hate you!" At which she backed him against the wall and slapped him. He did not speak to his mother again. The next morning, he ate his breakfast in sullen silence, and left for school without saying good-bye.

Now, because he was the oldest child and only son, he swore vengeance on whoever had snatched his mother from him and his sisters. No matter how long it took or how far he had to travel, he would track down her killer and bring him to justice. Jeff was a lawyer's son, not to mention a disciple of superheroes, so justice was a concept he knew something about. Justice meant holding a person accountable for his actions. Justice meant making a person answer for his crime. In everyday terms, justice meant courts, judges, juries, and lawyers—like his father and like Perry Mason, whom he also watched on TV and sometimes pretended to be, in make-believe with Patty and his best friend, Paul Erickson, as they rode their bikes up and down Hillcrest Avenue in search of wrongdoers.

But as he lay there, unable to sleep, his mind kept drifting back to what he thought of as eternity, to the mystery of never-ending time and boundless space. A vast emptiness like an enormous room seemed to have opened in front of him, and his mother had suddenly and unaccountably disappeared in it.

"I tried to comprehend never seeing my mother again," he wrote years later, when he was both a father and a lawyer. "She had always been there. Day in and day out. When I came home from school. When I went to sleep at night. Now I was never going to see her again, never going to talk to her again, and never is a long, long time."

3.

Life for the Thompson siblings would never be the same. A door had swung open, and they too had been swept, by a force they could not see or comprehend, from one room into another. Suddenly motherless, they were surrounded and sheltered by relatives and friends, yet the four of them often felt utterly alone, in a new and unordinary place.

Their father, maternal grandparents, and several aunts and uncles had quickly decided that life would be as normal as possible for the children. They would return to their own home—after Marj Young, Marian Erickson, and a handful of other close friends of their mother gave the place a thorough cleaning—and go back to school. To enforce the supposed normalcy, the adults imposed new rules in the home, banning newspapers, limiting exposure to television and radio, even forbidding the kids from answering the door and telephone. If a car pulled up when they were playing in the yard, they were not to respond to questions, comments, or requests to pose for snapshots. If a detective or reporter appeared at the door, an adult would see what he wanted. Even within the family, talk about their mother's death and the murder investigation was strictly prohibited.

Many years later, Margaret said Otto Swoboda once told her that he had hired "bodyguards" to keep a discreet eye on the siblings after the murder. There were reports of threats on the youngsters' lives and rumors of kidnapping-for-ransom schemes stemming, presumably, from all the talk about million-dollar insurance policies and Swoboda's status as a business owner, though police files contain no suggestion of such threats.

The children would remember nothing about threats and guards. And, whatever the adults' intentions, they were hardly prisoners of the new rules and restrictions. They attended classes, resumed music lessons, and were driven to Sunday school and scout meetings much as they had before their mother's death. They continued to play with their friends—albeit with greater adult supervision than they would remember having had in the past. Jeff, for his part, divided frequent visits to the Highland Village drugstore between the comic-book rack and the newsstand, torn between his beloved superheroes and the daily newspaper accounts of Lieutenant Barkley's investigation of his mother's death. Back at home, he surreptitiously shared what he learned and could understand about the investigation with his sisters.

The children of a popular and upstanding family, the Thompsons had always been treated well by friends and neighbors; now they were the object of unprecedented kindness and solicitude. Jeff and erstwhile classmates alike remember the kid gloves with which he was handled at s.p.a. following the murder. Margaret would recall a heightened attention from her playmates and their parents. "All of a sudden I was on everyone's hit parade," she said much later. "I was invited to parties I had never been invited to before."

"At first people were very gentle, very protective of us," Patricia said. "Both the kids and the adults."

Only later would the Thompsons understand that at least some of the attention they unaccustomedly basked in during those first several weeks after their mother's death was a mix of kindness, pity, and curiosity. Jeff and the girls were innocent victims of the most infamous crime in local memory and, as such, celebrities of an odd and particularly precious sort. People felt sorry for them, of course, but there was undoubtedly more to the response—such as the desire to be close to headline news, to the topic everybody was talking about, to living history. In St. Paul, in the late winter and early spring of 1963, there was nothing more prominently in the news, nor any more urgent topic of conversation, than the Thompson murder. For even the best-intentioned friends, the presence of a Thompson child at the dinner table would have been a coup, something to tell co-workers and relatives about. For the Thompson kids themselves, the situation was comparable to being the birthday boy or girl without having a birthday—fun and exciting, but confusing, too.

Then, as public suspicion of T. Eugene Thompson increased, the feelings toward his children—the nature of their celebrity, they would recognize in retrospect—began to change. Jeff would later recall sitting in the barber's chair while older customers debated whether "that Thompson guy" was involved in his wife's murder. In a letter he wrote to his father in 1996, he said, "Everyone had an opinion and felt free to discuss it, not knowing or caring if the children were listening."

Amy, despite her age at the time, would again claim especially vivid memories of the period. "People would invite me over for lunch," she said. "They'd feed me and be so nice—and then they'd tell me whether they thought my dad was guilty or not. People would drive up to the house, see me playing in the yard, and beckon me over. 'Oh, I'm so sorry about your mom,' they would say. And then they would tell me what a terrible person my dad was." Once in a while, house rules notwithstanding, one of the kids would pick up the telephone when it rang. "I remember answering the phone and people telling me what a horrible man my father was," Amy said, "and that apples don't fall far from the tree—whatever *that* meant. Of course, I didn't know what they were talking about."

What once may have been akin to being the center of attention at a birthday party had quickly become an unpleasant, frightening experience. Jeff said he felt "like a bug in a glass jar."

4.

Though T. Eugene had given up his downtown office, perhaps to save money, and begun working out of the house, the siblings saw no more of him than they did when their mother was alive. And that had not been much, at least by middle-class family standards of the time. Margaret recalled setting a place for him at the dinner table no more frequently than a couple of times a week.

T. Eugene was gone a great deal, supposedly taking care of legal business for his father-in-law's company and the village of North St. Paul (both of which retained his services through the summer and early fall of 1963), meeting with other clients or in court on clients' business, or on an out-of-town trip for this or that professional organization. When he was at home, his behavior was unpredictable and often bewildering, at least as far as the children were concerned. One day, for the benefit of a *Life* magazine photographer who had stopped by for "candid" pictures, he tossed a football back and forth with Jeff in the front yard. Jeff later insisted that that had been the only time the two of them had played catch on the lawn. Sometimes T. Eugene was visited by people the kids did not know, the visitors often arriving by taxi cab and conversing with their father in the dining room, which he now used as his office. On a few occasions, T. Eugene came home with a pretty woman in tow. He introduced the woman to the kids, but offered no explanation as to who she was or what she was doing in his company—at least not that the kids would remember years later. Sometimes he would show the woman around the house—as though the place had been for sale, or was a tourist attraction— before the two of them departed.

In the first few weeks after their mother's death, Geraldine Gesche, their father's sister, stayed at 1720 Hillcrest and tended to the house and children. A stolid, hardworking farmer's wife and mother of three children, she also positioned herself as a fire wall between T. Eugene and reporters, who called and presented themselves at the door several times a day during the first few weeks of the investigation, requesting interviews or comment. Mrs. Gesche summarily turned the reporters away. Later, when it became apparent that a more permanent presence was going to be needed, Thompson and Otto Swoboda hired a woman named Alta Grassinger to manage the home. "Everybody tried to keep things going on schedule, as if nothing had happened, even though the world had turned upside down," Jeff wrote later.

The Thompson kids would remember the presence of "Mrs. G" as one of the few happy developments of that miserable year. A chain-smoking, forty-something widow who once operated a catering service and had raised a son and foster daughter of her own, she could handle the logistics of the household at least as well as Carol or Aunt Geri had. More important, she quickly came to love the kids, and they loved her back. In fact, in retrospect, "homemaker"—as she was usually called—did not begin to describe her role and importance to the wounded family.

Patty was unwelcoming at first. "I guess I didn't really accept the fact that my mother was gone," she would recall. "Mrs. G was older than Mom, more like Grandma Swoboda's age, and it was hard to think of her taking my mother's place." But, soon enough, Mrs. G had worn down Patty's resistance. "She was a comforting, nurturing type," Patty said later. "She would let us come to her whenever we wanted to, and we would just sit there and she would hug us. She had an open heart."

Not surprisingly, Amy seemed to need those hugs the most. For many months after her mother's death, the little girl would climb out of bed at all hours of the night, creep into her sisters' room, and silently watch them breathe. She did not dream much about her mother during that period, but worried constantly about losing the rest of her family. She also fretted about Mrs. G. "I remember worrying that *she* would die," Amy said later. "But one time when I told her that, she told me she would never die, because she was a witch. She said, 'To prove it to you, I'll make the street lamp go out, anytime you say.' So I said, 'Okay, make it go out *now*.' And she pointed out the window at the street lamp—*and it went out*. It really did! Mrs. G always encouraged my fantasies. I'd tell her I just saw the Easter Bunny, and she'd say, 'Shhhh! You weren't supposed to see him!' I think she loved me best of all."

The kids spent a great deal of time with the Swobodas and the Zabels. The former had been especially important in the children's lives, as they had been in Carol's and Cotton's, and now, after Carol's death, they were the siblings' primary protectors and support.

Otto, an unfailingly generous soul, had been underwriting the household for almost fifteen years, providing a significant share of his son-in-law's professional business and financing the couple's successive homes. How he and Cotton agreed to split Mrs. G's compensation is not known, but it is quite likely that Otto saw to most of the expenses during the unsettled period between the murder and Thompson's conviction. (Whether he helped cover his son-in-law's legal bills before his conviction is not known, either.) There is no question that Otto took care of nearly everything for a long time after Thompson went to prison.

Swoboda was sixty-two years old when Carol died. His shock and grief were surely staggering, yet no one can remember an open display of emotion. If her murder changed him, as it surely did, his grandchildren and others who knew him at the time do not recall his being visibly or functionally diminished. Whatever inner turmoil he suffered, he always appeared steady, stoical, calm, and controlled. "I used to think he was kind of a wimp," Amy said, "because whenever you asked him a question, Grandma would answer and he would act as though that was perfectly all right. But I realized later that he was just a quiet man."

Outwardly, Toni Swoboda had been the stronger personality. Even less physically imposing than her husband, she was, nonetheless, a strict disciplinarian and unforgiving taskmaster who exposed her grandchildren to broad learning and high culture while holding them to rigorous personal standards. Though children wearied and often annoyed her, there was little doubt that the former schoolteacher cherished her grandkids, albeit with what would later be called "tough love." She was also, according to her granddaughters, a woman of wide-ranging spirituality, at least until her daughter died, combining a belief in reincarnation and the "other side" with her more conventional Presbyterianism.

Toni made the children memorize the names of the state capitals, inspirational poems, portions of great speeches, and extended Bible passages such as the Twenty-third Psalm. Personal virtue, intellectual discipline, and resourceful self-sufficiency were the objectives, and Toni's "teachers" ranged from Shakespeare ("Sweet are the uses of adversity. . .") to one Ralph Parlette, author of a book of received wisdom called *The University of Hard Knocks.* What is more, if life was a continuous lesson under her roof, learning had to be its own reward, because praise for the learner was rare. One day during his sophomore year at s.p.a., Jeff stopped by his grandparents' home to announce that he had won first prize in a science-project competition sponsored by the 3m Company. "Jeffrey Douglas Thompson," his grandmother responded, "sometimes you show signs of almost human intelligence."

After Carol's death, the Swobodas were content to be active—indeed, controlling—grandparents rather than surrogate parents, and to hire out the children's day-to-day supervision. T. Eugene's mother was dead, and his unhappy relationship with his father (who still lived in Elmore) apparently precluded the older man's involvement in family affairs. T. Eugene's surviving brother, Wallace, who practiced law in Winnebago, not far from Elmore, was never close to his nephew and nieces. Cotton's sisters and their families, however, continued to make frequent visits to Highland Park. Geri Gesche and her affable husband, Freeman, often took one or more of the kids back to their farm near Blue Earth. Just as Carol had enjoyed warm relations with Cotton's sisters, so, for the most part, did the Thompson kids.

Jeff and his sisters had lost their mother, but, as the spring of that year melted into summer, they did not want for caring adults in their lives.

5.

As soon as the school year was over in June, the children were whisked out of town, away from the newspapers and the gossips, to spend the summer at Forest Lake.

T. Eugene continued to come and go, a sometime presence in his children's lives, absent, in any case, more often than he was there. When he was at the lake, he was usually his old self, both fun-loving and domineering, eager to make the most of the family's boats and water skis. His use of the fifteen-foot runabout, in particular, was, as it had always been, manic to the point of recklessness. The siblings remember him revving up the boat's seventy-five-horsepower Mercury engine, racing across the water, and making abrupt, tight turns, laughing as the spray swept over the gunwales and drenched his passengers. Amy recalled one occasion after Carol's death when he took the kids out in the family's speedboat and let everyone have a swallow of beer—in what she later interpreted as a clumsy attempt at being a pal as well as a father. Occasionally, when Carol's memory was invoked, his eyes welled up and he would cry in front of the children.

Mrs. G was in charge of the kids that summer, driving them into the village of Forest Lake for treats and an occasional movie and providing warmth and comfort as their father and grandparents moved back and forth between the cabin and home. The siblings' teenaged cousin, Sharon Gesche, was a frequent baby-sitter, spelling Mrs. G, and the kids were allowed to invite friends up from the city for a visit. Once in a while an unfamiliar car would pull into the driveway and a stranger, sometimes with a backseat full of kids, would ask if this was the Thompsons' cabin. Sometimes the stranger would snap a couple of photos of the place before driving off.

It was the kind of sunny, salubrious getaway the siblings needed that summer. They undoubtedly suffered bad dreams and periods of heartache, as they had back home, but they would not remember that later. Despite their mother's absence, the summer of 1963 was remarkably close to normal in its lazy routines. In fact, decades later, only one day and night stood out in sharp relief from the muzzy, sun-splashed background against which they lived their lives that summer.

On June 20, cousin Sharon was nominally in charge at Forest Lake, and the day, as Jeff recalled it, began on an improbably positive note. Jeff's best friend, Paul Erickson, had come up from St. Paul to help celebrate Jeff's fourteenth birthday. Then, in what seemed to be a spectacular stroke of luck, the boys ran into Bonnie Bengel, Jeff's next-door neighbor from Highland Park, and one of Bonnie's friends in the village. The girls, it turned out, were also vacationing in the area. Though Bonnie was a year older than Jeff, she had been his "secret neighborhood heartthrob" for some time. Back at the cabin, the boys, after some adolescent dithering, decided to ask the girls to go to the movies that night. They would call them from a nearby grocery store, so they would not be overheard by Jeff's sisters.

Jeff pedaled the new ten-speed bicycle he had received from the Swobodas for his birthday. Paul kept pace on Patty's bike. But as they raced along the lakeside road, Paul, the bigger and stronger of the two, bumped Jeff onto the shoulder. Jeff's front tire caught in the sand. The bike came to an abrupt stop, and Jeff flew over the handlebars. His chest and arms were scraped raw. But, not about to blow the opportunity, he gamely remounted his bike and proceeded with Paul to the grocery store. They made the call and celebrated the girls' willingness to join them at the movies. The show they would see that night was *Miracle of the White Stallions*. Back at the cottage, as Jeff recalled the incident years later, Sharon gave him a shot of whiskey "for the pain" and tended to his wounds with soapy water and Mercurochrome.

After supper the boys primped for their dates. Despite the day's heat and his painful abrasions, Jeff put on a long-sleeved white shirt and black slacks, still not quite believing the stroke of luck that allowed him to spend a night on the town with Bonnie Bengel. When the boys arrived at the Forest Lake cinema, however, both girls made it clear, by their choice of seats, that they were more interested in Paul than in Jeff. Jeff was crestfallen, but not surprised. "Paul was five-ten, wore his hair long, and looked like Elvis Presley," he would recall. "I was a little fat kid who looked like a toad."

Jeff's wounds began to weep during the movie and, when the foursome emerged after the show, his white shirt was a bloody mess. Sharon and Patty came by in Mrs. G's Ford Falcon and drove the little party to the village A&W for root beer. Paul sat in back with Bonnie and her friend while Jeff, in his sticky shirt, slumped morosely up front with his cousin and sister. Then, at the drive-in, he administered his own coup de grace. Attempting to pass a large mug of root beer to the back seat, he clumsily dumped the soda on his head.

That night, sleepless in his bunk, Jeff burned all over and ached inside. It was, he decided, the second worst day of his life, and he wondered what else could have gone wrong.

Sometime after midnight he heard cars on the gravel driveway, a knock at the door, then the voices of his cousin and several men. He heard one of the men ask for his father and, when Sharon said that Mr. Thompson was not home, he heard the men ask to come inside. He may have dozed off. But perhaps an hour later he recognized the sound of his father's Oldsmobile in the driveway and then his father's voice in the living room. His father and the men were talking—calmly, it seemed, and in low tones, presumably so they would not wake the children in the adjacent rooms. Jeff could not make out, or would not remember, most of what the men said, but later recalled his father ask if this was necessary. "I would have come in if you wanted me," he heard his dad say.

His friend Paul and his sisters were sleeping. Jeff, however, lay wide-eyed and miserable in the prickly heat. Eventually, exhausted, he fell asleep. When he woke the next morning, his father was gone.

6.

In fact, T. Eugene was gone for only a couple of days before posting his $100,000 bail and resuming his irregular commutes between the Twin Cities and Forest Lake. His children would remember little of that part of the summer, though it is reasonable to assume that they were confused by their father's arrest and release.

The arrest itself seemed to be a terrible mistake. Jeff and the two older girls surely knew, from Jeff's surreptitious review of the newspapers at the Highland Village drugstore, that the police had been interested in their father, but it was not yet conceivable to any of them that their father could have been in any way responsible for their mother's death. Besides their predictable disinclination to imagine, let alone believe, that he had paid someone to kill her, their father and all the other trusted adults in their lives, from their grandparents, aunts, and uncles to their many friends and neighbors, seemed to reaffirm the idea that the murder had been the unexplainable act of an evil stranger.

Furthermore, the older kids, who had watched with their parents countless episodes of *Dragnet* and *Perry Mason*, believed that to be arrested was to go to jail. The idea of bail, if the process had been mentioned to them at all, would have been confusing. If their father had been arrested, what was he doing back at the cabin? But if the kids dared break the rules and ask one of the adults that question, they probably did not receive a candid answer. Chances are they never asked. For any number of reasons, including a few they would not appreciate until much later, it was easier not to ask, not to wonder about things they could not understand. Better to swim, play with their friends, and read the comic books they brought back to the cabin from their forays into town, and to try not to think about the rest of it at all.

When they returned to Highland Park for the start of the new school year, they were greeted, however, by an even more confusing reality. Many of their playmates and acquaintances—or, if not the kids themselves, their parents—were afraid of them. The ugly speculation that began in the spring had hardened into rock-ribbed conviction over the summer. Since T. Eugene had been arrested and charged in Carol's death, even many of the family's friends and neighbors had begun identifying the Thompson children with the accused murderer instead of with the victim.

"The arrest was the turning point," Jeff said later. "Everybody was pretty sympathetic to us, if not to my father, up till then. People were fascinated by the Thompson kids, interested in being involved with us, and supported us. After the arrest, people were uncomfortable and afraid not just of my father but of *us*. Even at s.p.a., where people had been very kind to me right after the murder, I had a much more limited number of friends than I had before my father's arrest." The children lost many of their playmates, whose parents did not want them associating with the Thompsons. Jeff's few close friends became fewer. Sometimes the kids themselves were hostile.

Patricia said, "After my father was arrested, people were mean. Kids would taunt us. Call us murderers. Ask us what we were doing there. 'We don't want you here,' they would say. 'We don't want murderers around here.' I tried to respond with a stiff upper lip. I told myself, 'Don't let them see you cry.' But it was hard. I didn't feel guilty about anything, and I didn't think my father was guilty of anything, and I couldn't understand why everyone was being so mean."

"We became pariahs," Margaret said. "It was as though there was suddenly a label on my forehead: MURDERER'S DAUGHTER. Like murder rubs off or something."

The fear and suspicion reached a crescendo when their father's trial began in October. No doubt nervous about what the increased attention and potential for abuse the trial would bring, their guardians, led by the Swobodas, did their best to isolate the children from the outside world, further constricting the pool of acquaintances who were permitted to play with them. Not surprisingly, the siblings drew closer together, believing that they had only each other for comfort and companionship.

Only seven years separated the four of them, but they had always been distinct individuals. Jeff now displayed the typical adolescent stew of anger, insecurities, and stirring hormones. Depending on his mood and the circumstance, he was his sisters' tormentor or paladin. Among the girls, Patricia was, according to the siblings' shared recollections, "Daddy's girl," "Princess Patty," "the one who always did the right thing." Margaret was rebellious and outspoken, with a mercurial, artistic temperament that accompanied her passion for music and dramatics. "We all hated Margaret," Jeff said later, laughing at the memory. "She was a prima donna, always wanting attention." Amy, the baby, was stubborn and gregarious. The siblings scrapped among themselves frequently, over petty things such as which TV show to watch or who would eat the last slice of cake, the more pugnacious Jeff and Maggie often joining forces against the righteous Patty. Still, photos from the late 1950s and early 1960s reveal more connectedness than contention, often with the two or three sisters in matching dresses made by their mother and big brother Jeff decked out in a sport coat and bow tie, standing protectively behind them. Now the foursome shared the murderer's mark.

Then, for a few moments in early December, Jeff shared the spotlight with his dad. He was a witness in his father's trial, answering questions about the morning his mother was murdered. Later, he would remember only fragments of the experience, unusual as it was for a fourteen-year-old boy. He would recall vague actions—walking down a hallway in the courthouse, entering the courtroom through a side door, thinking that the cramped, rather plain courtroom was not at all as he expected it to be, was nothing like the ornate chamber he was accustomed to seeing on *Perry Mason*. Everybody important except the judge and the jury was sitting at the same table: his father and his father's lawyers on one side, Mr. Randall, whom Jeff had seen only in the papers, and Randall's assistant on the other. The lawyers were sitting down, looking very relaxed, Jeff remembered, and they remained seated even when they asked him their questions. Not that he had a lot of time to observe his surroundings. He was in and out again in only a matter of minutes, and would not remember much more than that. Two things that did stay in his mind from the experience: The *Pioneer Press* would describe him in his S.P.A. uniform and polished shoes as "nattily clad." And, when he returned home from the courthouse, his father hugged him and gave him a watch.

The guilty verdict on December 6 that sent their father to prison the following morning was almost anticlimactic. Judging by newspaper stories the next day, few citizens had expected Thompson to go free. Meanwhile, the savvier and better-connected family friends such as Doug Young had prepared T. Eugene's supporters for the worst. By the trial's conclusion, only the defendant's siblings, in-laws, and closest friends held out hope for acquittal.

In their middle years, none of the Thompson children would be able to recall Doug Young's somber announcement on the evening of December 6, nor would they remember any encouraging or consoling words, hugs, or tears the last time they saw their father as a free man, which was probably a day or two before the verdict. Thompson spent the night of the sixth in the Hennepin County jail, from which he was transported directly to the state's maximum security prison in Stillwater the following morning. There was no chance to say good-bye.

7.

Perhaps the only surprising response to the verdict was the Swobodas'. Since the day of the murder, Otto and Toni had been unyielding in Cotton's defense, publicly and privately insisting on his goodness and innocence, testifying in court to his virtues as a husband and father, and apparently expecting a not-guilty verdict to the bitter end. But when the guilty verdict was read, their position collapsed. Overnight, T. Eugene ceased to exist in the Swoboda household. He was as dead to them in their hearts and minds as Carol was literally dead—actually, *deader*, since they would be loath to even acknowledge his memory. Toni cut Cotton's face out of family photos and refused to speak of him. As far as their grandparents were concerned, after December 6, 1963, the children's father was not only physically absent, he did not have a name.

"The moment the jury found Dad guilty, as far as our grandparents were concerned, he was not our father, he had nothing to do with us or we with him," Margaret said. "Grandpa told us that what Dad had done had nothing to do with us and didn't reflect on us. He had gone from white to black, believing that Dad was innocent and that the police always go after the husband or lover when a woman is murdered, to believing that Dad was dead. The man that Grandpa had loved and supported had died."

"We were tight before the murder," Amy said, summing things up with the hindsight of middle age. "But, afterwards, we were even tighter. For a while, it was just kind of us against them. Then it was, 'This is all you have.'"

The History Is Always There

1.

The disruptions, reversals, and abrupt, bewildering changes in the Thompson children's lives did not end when their father went to prison.

In some ways, the situation got worse. The united front maintained by the Swobodas and the Thompsons, for instance, crumbled when T. Eugene was found guilty of Carol's murder, and, at the beginning of the new year, the two sides were sharply divided. Otto and Toni Swoboda vehemently accepted the jury's verdict, while Thompson's sisters and brother just as vehemently did not, and the children, believing their father innocent while remaining both physically and emotionally close to their grandparents, were caught in between.

Then there was the issue of the children's custody.

Late in the day on January 5, 1964, a Sunday, Geraldine Gesche, T. Eugene's sister, arrived at 1720 Hillcrest and told Alta Grassinger that she could take the evening off. Aunt Geri said she would spend the night with the children and take them to school the next morning. Instead, according to papers filed later in Ramsey County district court, Mrs. Gesche, early on the morning of the sixth, drove all four kids to Faribault County and presented a petition to a probate judge in the town of Winnebago, where T. Eugene's brother, Wallace, practiced law. The petition had been signed by T. Eugene and Jeff Thompson (though Jeff would have no recollection of the petition decades later), and asked that custody of the children be given to Geri and Freeman Gesche. The judge signed an order granting the request.

That morning, the Ramsey County document continued, Otto and Toni Swoboda had expected to meet with Mrs. Gesche and Wally Thompson in the St. Paul office of the Swobodas' lawyer, to discuss permanent guardianship of the children. When Geri and Wally failed to appear, Otto called the Hillcrest number. After getting a busy signal, he drove to Highland Park, where he discovered an empty house and the phone off the hook. A note informed him that there had been an "emergency"; Mrs. Gesche had taken the children but would return with them later that day.

Geri's action brought to the surface the dispute over control of the children—and the estate that would eventually pass to them—that had been simmering since T. Eugene's arrest the previous June. His conviction, in December, had increased the urgency of a resolution. For their part, the Gesches had been repeating Carol's purportedly often-stated wish that, if something ever happened to her, the children would go to live on the Gesche farm, where the family had often visited in happier times. Carol believed, and had said as much more than once, Mrs. Gesche insisted, that "only Aunt Geri had both a home and heart large enough," in Mrs. Gesche's words, to accommodate Cotton and Carol's brood. The Swobodas were of the equally firm conviction that Carol would have wanted the children to stay together, in their city schools and with their city friends, in the neighborhood where they had always lived.

True to her word, Mrs. Gesche returned to St. Paul with the kids that Monday afternoon. But the following morning, again without consulting the Swobodas, she withdrew the girls from their Highland Park schools (Patricia had started junior high the previous September) and drove the three sisters to her Faribault County farm. The Thompson faction had decided that Jeff should stay in St. Paul under the Swobodas' guardianship and finish the school year at S.P.A. Not surprisingly, the Swobodas were outraged with both the plan and Mrs. Gesche's unilateral action. Otto promptly sought, and received, an order from a Ramsey County probate judge granting him temporary custody of all four children.

The custody fight was eventually settled in the grandparents' favor. In the meantime, Jeff lived with Mrs. G on Hillcrest and continued to attend classes at S.P.A., while the girls were shuttled between St. Paul and Blue Earth, attending class in the latter district until school let out for the summer, then joining their brother to spend summer vacation at Forest Lake. When the Swobodas were finally granted permanent custody of all four siblings, Otto moved them—and the essential Mrs. G—into another Highland Park house, this one on Howell Street, only a few blocks from the Hillcrest address. They would live there, at the Swobodas' expense, for the next several years.

Decades later, the siblings would speak with no bitterness toward either side in the interfamily dispute, believing that all parties had had their best interests at heart. They agreed, however, that keeping the four of them together through their high school years was the single most important decision made on their behalf. During the bizarre events surrounding what they would always refer to, albeit benignly, as their "kidnapping" by Aunt Geri, the most unsettling aspect seemed to have been the girls' separation from their brother. "I remember feeling so sorry for Jeff," Margaret said many years later. "We girls had each other. He didn't have anyone."

The siblings remained on mostly good, if not particularly close, terms with their father's sisters and their families. But they would forever be grateful to the Swobodas for keeping their broken family together.

2.

The Thompson case, meanwhile, continued to draw front-page headlines during the first half of 1964. In February, "middleman" Norman Mastrian went on trial in his hometown of Duluth, after his lawyers petitioned and received their own change of venue. It was another long, exhausting event, comprising almost eight weeks and ninety witnesses. Like Thompson, Mastrian pleaded not guilty, though, unlike Thompson, he did not testify on his own behalf. (Nor was Thompson called to testify.) Once again, Dick Anderson and the motley group of small-time hoods who had turned state's witnesses paraded to the stand for the prosecution, which was led, this time, by Bill Randall's assistant in the Thompson trial, Steve Maxwell. Finally, on April 10, after nearly thirteen hours of deliberation, the Duluth jury found Mastrian guilty of first-degree murder, and he, too, was sentenced to life in prison. (Before the establishment of sentencing guidelines in 1980, persons serving "life sentences" in Minnesota faced a mandatory twenty-five years—less eight years, if applicable, for "good time"—before they would be eligible for parole.)

On June 22, Anderson pleaded guilty to the same charge and was sent to join Thompson and Mastrian at Stillwater. A few days after he arrived there, however, Anderson abruptly recanted his trial testimony, saying that neither Thompson nor Mastrian was involved, and that he had murdered Carol Thompson while burglarizing the Thompson home. Then, a few days later, he recanted the recantation, insisting that his life had been threatened at Stillwater. He was transferred to a federal prison in Sandstone, Minnesota, and later transferred again, to the federal penitentiary in Leavenworth, Kansas. Little more would be heard from either Mastrian or Anderson until each was paroled twenty years later.

Thompson, who, with Mastrian, denied threatening Anderson with anything, settled into prison life. As befit his education and professional experience, he was eventually given a clerical job and a reasonable amount of freedom within the institution's thick stone walls. (Bob and Cole Younger, who rode with Jesse James and had come to grief during their ill-starred raid on a Northfield, Minnesota, bank in 1876, had been the state prison system's most notorious residents up till then.) Thompson continued, nonetheless, to insist that he was innocent of his wife's murder, which he blamed, most often, on Dick Anderson and an accomplice, usually Willard Ingram, and, at other times, on the "Mob," which, he suggested, had been either sending a warning or meting out revenge when they killed his wife.

Every so often for the next several years, Thompson and one of a series of prominent lawyers—including, very briefly, F. Lee Bailey, who had made his name winning Sam Sheppard's freedom on appeal and three decades later would be a member of O.J. Simpson's defense team—petitioned for a new trial. The several appeals—two, in 1969 and again in 1975, reached all the way to the United States Supreme Court, which refused to hear them—all came to naught. But the recurring actions insured that the world knew Thompson was alive and still proclaiming his innocence.

3.

By the end of 1964, when the Thompson case was no longer daily news, the Thompson children had finally begun to fade back into what would have to pass as anonymity. Life, though, was irrevocably changed.

The previous year's Christmas photo, presumably taken by Alta Grassinger or one of the Swobodas around the time of their father's conviction, shows the four siblings dressed as though for church and standing in front of the formal portrait of their mother that had accompanied all those newspaper and television stories during the previous nine months. The girls appear cheerful and self-possessed; only Jeff—looking owlish and unhappy in oversized, black-rimmed glasses and his s.p.a. blazer—is not smiling. Whoever arranged the photo was clearly trying to create a picture of family unity, but the children, standing close together in a tight quartet, do not relate in any way to their mother's likeness that hangs on the wall above the mantel behind them. ("The shrine," as Jeff sometimes referred to it.) There is no reminder of their absent father. In the family's 1964 holiday portrait, Mrs. G, wearing a festive red sweater, sits front and center among the kids. Her arms enfold Margaret and Amy, Patty and Jeff stand close behind, and only a sliver of Carol's portrait is visible on the table beside them.

Years later, the children would remember few, if any, visits to their mother's tomb. If the Swobodas visited the cemetery, they did not take the children, or the visits did not make a lasting impression. And although the three oldest siblings knew their father was at Stillwater, they were not encouraged to visit, write, or speak to him on the phone. The adults told Amy that her father was sick and would have to spend a long time in a hospital. At least for a while, Jeff and her sisters went along with the story, and Amy was content to believe it.

One of the few sources of sunshine during the first years of their parents' absence was Mrs. G. By the siblings' accounts many years later, their live-in "homemaker"—"governess," as she was sometimes called in the papers, was too grand a description for the plainspoken Mrs. Grassinger—provided the nurturing center of their daily life after their mother died. Her own daughter was a frequent and sunny presence in the house as well—"Big Pat" to Patricia's "Little Pat." Mrs. G would have had to have been a reasonably strict and tidy housekeeper to remain in Otto Swoboda's employ for as long as she did, but what the kids remembered decades later was her generous, positive, and loving nature. Patricia remembered Mrs. G, the erstwhile caterer, inviting people "who didn't have anywhere else to go" for Thanksgiving and Christmas dinners at the Thompsons' table. "I loved that," Patty recalled. "We had never experienced that sort of kindness to strangers, and it was great."

Among the siblings themselves, Jeff remained the leader. He had been the leader for as long as his sisters could remember, and, by his own reckoning, for a long time prior to the watershed events of 1963. Decades later, he distinctly remembered baby-sitting his sisters when Amy was a toddler, while his parents played bridge, attended a play, or enjoyed dinner out with friends, though he was only eight the first time. If now, in his early teens, he was headstrong and overbearing—which by general agreement he definitely was—he was also, literally and by default, the man of the house. He was a temperamental mentor who taught Amy the game of chess and then angrily upended the board when she beat him, and a grumpy yet dutiful protector who would sit up and wait for the older girls to come home from the movies.

He was a bully and a tease. He loved to burst into the room during tense moments in a scary movie on TV, and, during outings at Forest Lake, hold his sister's head under water a heartbeat or two longer than everybody else thought was funny. In that sense, he reminded the girls of their father. But, unlike their dad, Jeff was always one of them, was there for them when they needed him, and, in Amy's words years later, "would in the end always do the right thing."

"He was our warrior," said Patty.

4.

Always a loner, with only a handful of friends among his classmates, Jeff eventually settled in at S.P.A. He wrestled competitively, played junior varsity football, and performed with the school's drill team. His powers of focus and concentration increased as he matured, and his grades were eventually good enough to earn him acceptance at both Stanford University in California and Carleton College in Northfield, Minnesota. Moving beyond the superheroes he had grown up on, he was increasingly preoccupied with the comely girls who seemed to be everywhere he looked. He loved the music of Roy Orbison, Chuck Berry, Buddy Holly, and other rock 'n' roll icons he had been listening to since he was a little boy. He listened endlessly to his mother's 45 RPM recordings of "Mean Woman Blues" and "Brown-Eyed Handsome Man," and took guitar lessons with the starry vision of someday playing in a rock 'n' roll band. He often thought about his mother. He was haunted by his angry words the day before her murder and by his refusal to speak to her on the final morning of her life, wondering, despite his better judgment, if he were somehow responsible for her death. But he tried not to dwell on her death and its aftermath. Gradually, his fantasies of superheroic vengeance faded. He had no interest, at least not early on, in becoming a lawyer like his dad.

He could not recall, as a middle-aged man, the first time he visited his father in prison. Early on, he was driven there by relatives on the Thompson side of the family, possibly without the Swobodas' knowledge and approval. When he was legally old enough to drive himself—he turned sixteen in June 1965—he began making the thirty-minute trip between St. Paul and Stillwater more often, eventually going out at least once every couple of months. He enjoyed, from the beginning of their lives under his grandparents' regime, significantly greater independence and freedom than his sisters did, and, once he had his driver's license and his own car, he more or less came and went as he pleased.

The prison visits were an odd, even surreal, experience. Years later, Jeff remembered driving out State Highway 36, parking among the other visitors' cars, walking up to the huge, stone edifice, and passing through the locked and guarded gates. Amid a gaggle of sundry visitors—most of whom were wives and girlfriends of inmates and their small children—he was almost always the only unaccompanied teen. He would check in, wait for his father to be summoned from his work detail or cell, and then join T. Eugene in a large room with tables and chairs, a gray-blue haze of cigarette smoke, and the buzz of multiple conversations occasionally punctuated by a baby's squall. There were no bars or glass partitions separating the visitors from the prisoners, no need to use a telephone or speak through a grate. But there was no forgetting where they were. An unsmiling guard sat watchfully on a platform, and visits were limited to an hour.

At first, a certain excitement attached itself to the trek. Most people knew about prisons only via television shows and movies. But the state prison at Stillwater was the real thing, an actual "big house," with real guards at the gates and in the towers guarding real prisoners in the yards and cell blocks. Soon enough, though, the novelty had worn off, and the visits became a chore, something Jeff, and later his sisters, came to dread. Although they refused to believe that their dad was a murderer, they were not energized by feelings of outrage and injustice. Such emotions, at any rate, would not have been stimulated or encouraged by the Swobodas or even by their father's family, who, since the conviction, had taken a "less said, the better" stance, at least as far as the children were concerned. The youngsters' attitude, as best they could describe it later, was fatalistic. *Our mother was murdered, our father is in prison. That's our life, and there's nothing we can do to change it.* Their father, moreover, was a vital, persuasive, and charismatic man, even as a lowly clerk-typist in prison khakis. Unlike his own siblings, he was not reluctant to talk about the case, relentlessly insisting on his innocence and demanding the family's loyalty and affection. The visits, and occasional correspondence, were thus, to all intents and purposes, obligatory. Jeff would later compare the prison trips to visiting a relative in a cancer ward.

In fact, the siblings' responses to "our life" varied. Jeff would visit his dad with some regularity over the next twenty years. Patricia and Margaret began their separate visits when they were old enough to come and go without their grandparents' approval, sometimes accompanied by friends, sometimes by their father's kin, though the girls visited far less frequently than Jeff did.

The first time she went to Stillwater, Patricia stood in the visitors area waiting for her father to appear. She spotted a man emptying the ashtrays. Only when the man looked in her direction did she realize that it was her dad. "I don't think he was embarrassed for us to see him that way," she said later. "We would sit and chitchat, and then the conversation would get around to how he'd been falsely accused and convicted, and he'd give us all these so-called facts about those two guys [Anderson and Ingram] and the Mafia or whatever. At the time, I still believed he was innocent, so I tended to believe what he was saying. I thought it was terribly unfair, but, to be honest, I also think I was kind of relieved he was there. I didn't know why I felt that way at the time, so, of course, I felt guilty about that."

Margaret, who did not visit her father until she was eighteen, was surprised when she saw him for the first time in almost ten years. "I was really curious," she said later, "because from the time I was about ten, he was always described as this hideous, horrible monster. At the same time, there was this other message I was receiving all the while: 'You're a lot like him.' When she was still able to talk about him—meaning before his conviction—Grandma always said that Dad, Jeff, and I had a lot of similarities. So when I went to see Dad that first time, it was sort of a relief. He was intelligent. He was funny. We laughed at the same things. I thought he looked like an older Jeff. I remember sitting on a sofa in the visiting room, waiting for Dad to arrive. There were vending machines and guards. I felt it was a very hostile, very negative environment. But the man who appeared—I knew him. He wasn't a monster. He was a person I knew."

Amy, in her middle teens and disabused of the "hospital" fiction by that time, went to Stillwater only once. Later, she said that she had built up a larger-than-life, even heroic image of her long-absent father, whom she had trouble remembering as flesh and blood. When she finally saw him in prison, she was crestfallen. He was so much "smaller," so much more ordinary-looking and familiar, than she had expected.

The siblings were convinced that they were subjected to more red tape and longer waits than other prison visitors, possibly owing to their father's notoriety and his frequent appeals for a new trial. Thompson was, by most accounts, a model prisoner during most of his incarceration, but that did not mean he was liked by his keepers.

For nearly twenty years, Jeff visited his father in the main prison at Stillwater, the adjacent prison farm, and, later during the older man's sentence, in the more relaxed environs of the minimum-security facility at nearby Lino Lakes. Physically, T. Eugene changed over the period, as he put on weight and let his thick, graying hair grow out in bangs and bushy sideburns, reflecting the fashion of the outside world. As technological advances revolutionized office work, Thompson had acquired data-entry and other skills with the institution's rudimentary computers.

One day, T. Eugene introduced Jeff to an attractive woman named Vicky Miller, who happened to be visiting at the same time. Jeff said hello and waited for her to excuse herself a few minutes later. He would eventually discover that his dad had several female visitors, in addition to his sisters and daughters, over the years. Jeff would also encounter members of a small, inchoate band of men and women who believed T. Eugene was an innocent man wrongfully imprisoned. Most of those ad hoc supporters had not known T. Eugene before his conviction, but now they called, exchanged letters, and were eventually added to the prisoner's authorized-visitor list. The new friends were from diverse backgrounds and situations, apparently having in common little more than a belief in Thompson's innocence. One man, Dwight Culver, was a sociology professor at the College of St. Catherine in St. Paul. Culver was particularly zealous on T. Eugene's behalf, helping track down sources and other materials that Thompson would include in his serial appeals. Jeff bumped into Culver on more than one prison visit, and later recalled being bemused by the professor's passion for his father's cause.

Once when Jeff was visiting, Norman Mastrian happened to be in the visitors' room. Jeff had never seen the man in the flesh. Mastrian was surprisingly small, Jeff thought, but the former prizefighter had been lifting weights and, despite his size, that day seemed muscular and menacing. Jeff had recently decided on a career in law and took the opportunity to tell his dad of his plans. Thompson promptly relayed the news to Mastrian, who was sitting nearby. "Oh, that's terrific," sneered the latter. "Just what the world needs—another lawyer."

(Margaret would recall her own encounter with Mastrian, who, she said, told her she looked nice one day when he spotted her in the visiting area. Afterward, T. Eugene sharply instructed her not to talk to the man.)

Sometime later, after a handgun and liquor were discovered among Thompson's possessions, Jeff visited his father in the prison's segregation area. (T. Eugene insisted, to no avail, that the contraband had been planted among his things, in retaliation for his continuing appeals.) Jeff would remember the site as a grim, depressing, cacophonous space where the prisoner had no privacy or quiet. Jeff, though he was by that time a lawyer and probably thus permitted the visit, was shaken by the experience.

"It was a terrible place," he recalled. "I felt sorry for him in there."

5.

While Jeff matured and eventually flourished at s.p.a., his sisters progressed through the St. Paul public schools. Patricia spent one unhappy year at a church-based academy in Minneapolis, then returned to Highland Park, where she completed high school. The girls attended church at Edgcumbe Presbyterian, and their parents' friends looked in on them from time to time. Holidays were celebrated with the Swobodas. Summer vacations were spent at the lake.

Then, in May 1967, two weeks before Jeff's high school graduation, the siblings' life took another wrenching turn. One night, a commotion roused them from their sleep. Watching from their bedroom doors, they saw ambulance attendants wheeling Mrs. G down the hall on a stretcher. She had suffered a fatal aneurism. The siblings knew that she was a heavy smoker and enjoyed a drink from time to time, but they never thought of her as sickly or vulnerable, and her sudden death shocked them to the core. "I cried and cried," Amy, who was in fifth grade at the time, recalled.

"I really loved her. I knew her better than I'd known my mom."

After four years with Mrs. G, the children were briefly cared for by a young Edgcumbe pastor, Gary Hickok, and his family, then were joined by a St. Paul fireman named William Benz, his wife, Lorraine, and their two teenaged daughters. For the Thompson girls, the later period would be a time of almost constant conflict with their caretakers. To make matters worse, when Jeff began his freshman year at Carleton College in Northfield, forty-five minutes away, the girls were left to fend for themselves. Margaret, who was the same age as one of the Benzes' daughters and felt she was always at a competitive disadvantage in the household, had an especially difficult experience, and spent as much time as she could with the Swobodas. Patty was out of the house as often as she could manage and, eventually, departed for college herself. Bereft of Mrs. G, Amy tried to run away from home before finally moving in with her mother's aunt, Helen Zabel. Snapshots from the three years following Alta Grassinger's death reveal a progression of fashions, hairstyles, and moods as the visibly maturing siblings posed with the Benzes in front of the Howell Street house and on the shore of Forest Lake. Now, only Jeff, a dapper and somewhat cocky-looking young man visiting from college, appears to be even remotely happy.

The siblings remained close to their maternal grandparents. Positive and forward-thinking, Otto, who financed his grandchildren's stay with the Benzes, encouraged Jeff in his studies and urged the girls to take advantage of their individual strengths, with the long-term objective of making a happy and prosperous career and marriage. The siblings, for their part, loved Otto without reservation. They understood and appreciated his providential role in their lives and tried hard to please him, even as they increasingly chafed under his control. They loved Toni, too, but she was more difficult to deal with. She could not move on from her daughter's death.

Though she and her granddaughters listened to the opera on the radio and went shopping for school clothes as they had in the past, the girls realized that Toni had abandoned her once-powerful spirituality and religious faith and was hopelessly preoccupied by the murder. Talk about the case was forbidden among the children, but Toni spoke of it obsessively, even with total strangers, often introducing one or another of the red-faced girls to a nonplussed waitress or department-store clerk, and then recounting the story in painful detail.

More often than not, of course, the waitress or clerk was already familiar with the tale, including the gruesome particulars. As Patricia said later, "The history was always there. It was the reality we would have to live with." The siblings' once comfortably common name itself had become, for many Minnesotans of the period, synonymous with their mother's murder and their father's crime. "Oh, are you related to T. Eugene Thompson?" the children were asked on countless occasions, in disparate settings, the recollection invariably, they would note, centering on their father, not on their mom. "I was always T. Eugene's daughter, never Carol's," Margaret remarked.

Reminders of their troubled past would turn up unexpectedly. One day in 1969, Jeff was passing the Highland Village shopping center near home. In a bookstore window was a large display of Donald Giese's new book, *The Carol Thompson Murder Case.** As Jeff

---

* The St. Paul newspaperman's straightforward recounting of the Thompson case, from Carol's homicide through the convictions of Mastrian and Anderson the following year, has long been out of print. Copies still turn up, however, at Twin Cities garage sales and secondhand bookstores. Not long before the book's publication, Giese became a player in his own story, when he was called to testify during one of T. Eugene's several appeals. Thompson's attorney asked Giese to reveal

stood transfixed on the sidewalk, staring at the display, his mother's smiling face, multiplied a dozen times, stared back at him through the glass.

Sometimes the past would merge gratingly with the present, connecting the siblings, despite the best efforts of their grandparents, with their father in prison. One day, when Patty was about fifteen, she received a letter from T. Eugene. A few sentences into the note she realized that she was not its intended recipient. "Dad had a girlfriend who was also named Patricia," she said later. "He apparently wrote to the two of us at the same time and got the envelopes mixed up. I was so shocked! I showed it to Jeff, who read it and burned it. A little while later, the other Patricia called and asked if I had her letter. I wouldn't talk to her."

The girls wondered how much to tell prospective boyfriends about their family and their past, knowing that the information had already cost them so many relationships. When the subject of their parents came up among those rare individuals who did not know the story, the easiest response was to say, simply, "My mom is dead, and my dad is away." But sometimes that was not enough.

Once, when Patricia was about to bring a new boyfriend home to meet her siblings, she told him, "There's something you should know, and I want to tell you before you hear it from someone else. My father is in prison for hiring someone to kill my mom."

"Oh, bullshit," the young man scoffed.

"It's not," Patty said.

---

sources he had used while covering the case in 1963. When Giese refused, invoking journalistic tradition and the First and Fourth Amendments of the U.S. Constitution, a district court judge cited him for contempt and sentenced him to ninety days in jail. The Minnesota Supreme Court threw out the citation. Giese died, reportedly following a heart attack, in 1975. He was forty-seven.

The next day he told her, "You know, you're right. I went to the library and looked it up."

To their dismay if not surprise, the case's shadow would follow Patricia and Margaret to the private women's school in Columbia, Missouri, where Otto sent them after high school. Not long after Patty's arrival at Stephens College in the fall of 1969, a girl in her freshman dorm approached her and said, "I know who you are."

Patty drew a blank. She had never seen the girl before, so what could the girl know about her? "Okay," she replied. "Who am I?"

"You're T. Eugene Thompson's daughter," crowed the stranger, who explained that she had grown up in northern Minnesota, near Otto's hometown, and that her parents had known the Swoboda family. The girl then told whoever would listen the sensational story of Carol Thompson's murder and T. Eugene's conviction.

The crime, indeed, had an absurdly long shadow, even following Patty to east Africa, where she and some friends were enjoying a photographic safari after her graduation from college. "Thompson?" another traveler, who happened to be from Minnesota, exclaimed when they were introduced. "You didn't have anything to do with that murder back home, did you?"

6.

Otto Swoboda would help his grandchildren financially through their college years. But the son and daughters—and grandson and granddaughters—of hardworking achievers, the siblings were able and willing to make their own way in the world. In 1973, they received a bittersweet, one-time windfall, when the several companies that had insured their mother agreed to an out-of-court settlement of almost $450,000; after the lawyers took their cut and miscellaneous expenses were deducted, each of the four received about $60,000. (Despite his own legal efforts, T. Eugene received nothing.)

Happy to get away from Highland Park, Patty studied art education in college, with the objective of becoming a teacher. Margaret, a self-taught chanteuse who dreamed about a show business career, had pleaded to go to the Juilliard School of Music in New York, but her grandfather would have none of that, insisting that she follow Patty to Stephens and prepare for a business career, without the obvious distractions—and, no doubt in Otto's mind, the potential dangers—of a coeducational institution in the big city. They finally reached a compromise of sorts: Margaret went off to Stephens, but would study vocal performance and psychology.

A week after her eighteenth birthday, Amy and her sisters saw Elvis Presley in concert at the St. Paul Auditorium, then Amy set out by herself for California. A self-described "flower child," she had not done as well in high school as her sisters. Despite her grandfather's pleas that she further her education, and his promise to provide a free ride to any college she could get into, she had another, more singular objective in mind: She would be Alice in Wonderland at Disneyland. She almost landed the job, too, auditioning and then surviving several callbacks before the role was given to somebody else. In no hurry to return home, she worked a series of odd jobs and hung around southern California for a year.

At Carleton, Jeff majored in sociology, competed on the school's wrestling team, and helped organize student marches against the Vietnam War. He also fathered a child by his girlfriend, whom he married while they were both still undergraduates. He put food on the table by working as a janitor and delivery-truck driver. Upon graduation in 1971 and the expiration of his college deferment, with the Vietnam War at its height, he drew a high enough lottery number to escape the military draft. When, on a whim, he tried to enlist, he was rejected after admitting that he had thought about suicide during college and was informed by an army psychiatrist that he had a "problem with authority."

With no more exciting prospects in front of him, he decided that his past had, if nothing else, prepared him for a career in criminal justice. He did well on the LSAT and was admitted to the William Mitchell College of Law, the night school his father had attended when it was known as the St. Paul College of Law. In the fall following his graduation from Carleton, he started at Mitchell and, balancing full-time employment with his evening classes, managed to finish his first year ranked tenth in a class of almost three hundred. For a time while at Mitchell, he clerked for the Ramsey County District Court, where, coincidentally, both Hyam Segell, his father's erstwhile defense attorney, and Stephen Maxwell, who had assisted William Randall in his father's prosecution, were now judges. "They were all buddies," Jeff said later, referring to both sides of the counsel table at his father's trial, but neither Segell nor Maxwell, if they noticed him at all, paid Jeff any special attention.

Before he completed his law studies, Jeff and his wife divorced, and Jeff assumed custody of their son, who was four and a half at the time. "I was ready for the responsibility," he said later. "I had been, in effect, a single parent since I was thirteen. Now I actually had a child of my own." Luckily, he had also acquired, along with the parenting skills, a deep appreciation of irony and the absurd that would serve him well as an adult. Not long after he and his wife decided to part, he told T. Eugene, during a visit to Stillwater, that his marriage was over.

"Well, Jeffrey," T. Eugene told his son, "you know we don't believe in divorce in this family."

Jeffrey laughed. "No, we believe in murder," he replied. "But I'm going to start a new tradition—a less drastic alternative."

On his own again, and responsible only for himself and his son, Jeff joined a small St. Paul law firm; then, after a year of private practice, took a job as an assistant county attorney in Winona, a city of almost 30,000 in the southeast corner of the state. Jeff was interested in criminal defense law by that time and felt the best way to acquire experience was in prosecution. As it turned out, he spent three years as an assistant prosecutor, handling the beginner's usual complement of DWI's and shoplifting cases.* Beginning in 1979, he practiced criminal defense and family law in Winona, trying a couple of murder cases from the other side of the table, before coming to the realization—at Christmastime 1985—that prosecution best suited him after all. "I wouldn't have to worry about clients, and I wouldn't have to worry about all the lies and obfuscation," he explained later. "I could just try to do the right thing." His domestic life, in the meantime, followed its own zigzag course. While in Winona, he remarried, then, five years later, divorced, and, a couple of years after that, married for a third time. With his third wife he would have two more sons.

Following her college graduation, Patty moved to Kansas City with a girlfriend, planning to get a job teaching school. Before that happened, however, she picked up a handsome hitchhiker who, it turned out, was a sous chef at a Kansas City hotel and shared her passion for cooking. While seeing each other during the next two weeks, the two of them fell in love and decided to marry. A justice of the peace performed a desultory ceremony, and Patty phoned her family with the news. Her siblings were disappointed that they had not had a chance to be part of a wedding. Just as predictably,

---

* During Jeff's employment in the Winona County attorney's office, his boss, Julius Gernes, prosecuted one Donald Howard for the 1977 murder of Howard's wife, Shirleen. In a high-profile case with eerie similarities to T. Eugene Thompson's, Howard, who had been seeing another woman, was convicted of having hired a hit man to kill his wife in the basement of their Winona home while Howard took their two young daughters shopping. The murder was supposed to look like an accident. After serving twenty-two years in prison, Howard was paroled in 2000.

Otto was shocked and upset. "He wanted us to have a big wedding," Patty recalled. "And he hadn't had a chance to check out my husband." A year later, Patty had a baby, and the couple settled down in the Twin Cities.

The family eventually moved to South Canaan, Pennsylvania, where Patty's husband began studying to be a Russian Orthodox priest. Living on Patty's share of her mother's insurance money, the couple grew their own vegetables and rented a farm house reputed to have briefly been "home" to Patricia Hearst following her abduction by the Symbionese Liberation Army in 1974. ("That's what everyone around there said," Patty remarked later. "But I'm so sensitive to trauma, I think I would have picked up on it if it was.") By that time, the couple was not getting along, so Patty, tired of supporting her husband, took their daughter back to Minnesota and, after less than four years of marriage, filed for divorce. She later became a middle-school teacher in the Minneapolis public school system.

Margaret's post-college history was only somewhat less volatile. She returned to the Twin Cities from Missouri with degrees in music and psychology. For a time she sang in local supper clubs and an occasional musical production. But Otto, still a powerful influence in her life, encouraged her to make the most of her native math skills and "affinity for systems." She went to work in the accounting office of the Minneapolis-based Dayton Hudson department-store chain, and, later, on information systems, at Dayton Hudson's bookselling subsidiary. There she fell in love with a manager from Colorado named John Wilson. A month after they met, he proposed, and, four months later, they were married. The couple eventually divorced; then they were married again and had a son and a daughter.

Amy, whom her siblings by this time were calling the "wild child," returned home after her year on the West Coast, attended a trade school, and worked for a couple of years as a travel agent. Bored, she took a job working the night shift behind the front desk of a motel in Golden Valley, a Minneapolis suburb. One evening, a smooth-talking guest named Doug Simmons impressed her. Simmons sold Gulf of Mexico shrimp off the side of a truck, moving from one city to another, returning south for more inventory, then coming back up north to sell it. "He was a character, a bit of a con man, and he had been in jail," Amy said later. He was also twenty-nine years older than she was—about the same age as her father. A week after their first date, she moved in with him. Then she quit her job and joined him on the road. They married and settled in Shreveport, Louisiana, his hometown. She was twenty-four.

"I loved Doug blindly," Amy said. "He had a lot of faults and was sort of a rake. But he was a hedonist—a lot like me. He had been bad when he was young—a thief—but he would never dream of hurting anyone. He was always open with me and never tried to hide anything. By the time I met him, he was definitely trying to do right in life."

Amy's siblings interpreted Doug Simmons's appeal as, at least partly, that of a surrogate father, which, with some qualification, Amy herself would not deny.

7.

In March 1981, T. Eugene was the subject of a long, two-part feature in the *Minneapolis Tribune*. Thompson had spent more than seventeen years in prison and been denied his first petition for parole. Corrections officials and prison visitors, including the occasional journalist, variously described him as a quiet, well-behaved prisoner and a shadow of his former cocksure self, and a clever fellow—cleverer, at any rate, than most of the "cons" around him—who knew how to make the most of his situation. He had been assigned a series of "office jobs" and enjoyed more autonomy than many of his fellow inmates. Staff writer Eric Black noted that Thompson was fifty-three "and looks it. The blond flat top has been replaced with a fuller head of gray hair. He sports a neatly trimmed moustache." Thompson was not wearing glasses in the accompanying photos, and his eyes were pouched and tired-looking. Instead of the stylish suits, tab-collar shirts, and coordinated accessories of earlier appearances in the local papers, he wore, according to Black, a plain knit sport shirt and jeans. He was no longer, for that matter, the "prominent attorney" of eighteen years earlier, having been disbarred following his conviction.

Some things had not changed. Black's feature made clear that Thompson was the same voluble self-apologist last heard declaiming at length during his trial, still given to the kind of overblown explanations that reminded *Tribune* readers of his speeches from the witness stand nearly two decades earlier. He was also as insistent about his innocence as ever—and, apparently, just as eager to argue his case. According to Black, Thompson arrived for the interview carrying a "briefcase full of documents" and a "tape recorder to record his own remarks."

"Now, when you first come to prison, you're in a cell that you've never been in before," the inmate lectured his visitor. "It's six feet by nine feet, contains a sink and a stool and a bunk in the wall and a flop-down little metal top called a desk. And a chair, a wooden chair. And that's it."

Thompson spoke at length, and with passion, about waiting the seventeen years a prisoner in Minnesota had to wait at that time to be eligible for parole, and then the surprise and disappointment of the request being turned down. "I can't imagine any reason for me not to be released," he said. "When you examine all the positive aspects, is it possible that they are going to have a person more eligible for parole than me? Fine, if there is, but if you examine my background, education, experience, training, and record, it would be very difficult to do better." He spoke about the deprivations of prison life, especially during the first few years of the sentence: "You feel like you're in a cocoon, with no means of communication. You are totally isolated." When he talked about his children, Black said, his face clouded over and his voice cracked. "You are utterly, totally helpless. . . . You can't do anything for your children except pray and write letters," the prisoner said, and began to cry. "You'd think it wouldn't bother me any more after all these years," he added tearfully. "But it does."

In part two of the interview, Thompson reiterated his claim that Dick Anderson was a murderer and a liar, that he himself was too smart to have tried to orchestrate the foolish scheme that had been attributed to him, that the state suppressed exculpatory evidence during his trial, and that political considerations were keeping him from receiving the new trial that he had been seeking for almost seventeen years. That was to say, presumably, that the governor and various appellate court judges did not have the backbone to make what would have been a hugely unpopular decision to see justice done in the case of the state's most notorious prisoner.

Thompson told Black that he had never asked his kids to believe that he was innocent of their mother's murder. Early on, he said, he told them that he understood that they were "being raised probably with the concept that your father's in prison because he deserves to be, and that he's guilty." But, he said he told them, "I want you to know that I did not kill your mother." He acknowledged that it had surely been difficult for the children growing up under the cloud of his conviction. During their visits and other communication, he said, "I'd ask questions, try to draw them out on it. But I'd be careful not to ask too many. Kind of let them come along at their own pace as the years passed. But it was rough, very rough."

Jeff Thompson was thirty-one in March 1981, a lawyer in private practice in Winona. Contacted by Black for the story, he spoke carefully but at length about his experience as T. Eugene's son. He said that while it had not been a "conscious decision" to follow his father into law, he did not "think it was a coincidence, either." He said, "I think my background has led me naturally to be interested in law regarding families and regarding crimes." He spoke of the discomfort of living in the public eye following his mother's murder, but he revealed no self-pity or bitterness and was reluctant to assign blame.

> I can't think of anybody offhand who consciously gave me a hard time . . . but I felt the adverse effects of it. Everybody bends over backwards to be objective and fair about it, but I detected a lot of undue pressure on myself. . . . I never blamed my father for it. I never blamed anybody for it. It's just fate. I never thought of it as my father's fault. . . .
>
> Once I was riding the bus to law school, something about my dad was in the paper that day, and I heard two women talking about it, how terrible it was, [and] that they hoped he would never get out of prison. [But] to this day, even now, in Winona, people will come up to me and say, "We never thought your dad was guilty."

One day, Jeff told Black, while visiting Winona's public library, he picked up one of its two copies of Giese's book. The card inside the back cover indicated that *The Carol Thompson Murder Case* had been checked out no fewer than sixty times during the previous year.

Jeff talked about the visits and telephone calls that he and his sisters made to his father in prison. Despite the difficulty of seeing him "under those kind of circumstances," Jeff said, he was always "eager to talk and communicate" with his dad. "He is a most articulate and understanding person. He's compassionate. He gives me good advice." As for his and his sisters' belief in their father's innocence or guilt, he responded with an equanimity that probably baffled many readers:

> It's not even a good question. There's no special knowledge that the children have. To a large extent it doesn't really make any difference [what we think]. We've been propagandized from both sides enough that mostly we just don't think about it too much.
>
> He's our father. He was a good father when he was living with us. He's just a person. He's got his faults and he's got his good points. We don't discuss and don't even think about his guilt or innocence.
>
> We did all go and support his request for parole. We certainly don't think he's any danger to society. We emotionally don't believe [the verdict]. I'm convinced that the trial was not an accurate portrayal of what happened. We are not convinced that the explanation that the state provided of what happened is correct.
>
> If [my sisters and I] could have our fondest wish, there isn't one of us who wouldn't really love to know what really happened then. But I guess I'm satisfied that it's a question that will never be answered to my satisfaction. It's too confusing.
>
> Most people are going to create an image of T. Eugene Thompson and his kids that has no connection with reality. We've learned that as long as we're honest with ourselves, we can live with the things people say about us.

Asked, finally, if he thought about taking over his father's continuing appeals, Jeff conceded that he had been feeling "a lot of pressure" to join the fight. (Pressure from whom he did not say.) Nevertheless, he said, "I just don't feel like I'm ready to do it."

8.

Jeff never did add his name to the list of T. Eugene Thompson's attorneys, but, in December 1982, almost two years after that interview in the *Tribune*, he wrote a letter to Minnesota corrections officials in support of his dad's third parole petition. Jeff argued that his father was not a threat to public safety, quoted the Lord's Prayer on the subject of forgiveness, and concluded with a dramatic plea: "Please, let my father go!"

Whether the letter tipped the balance or not, a week later state corrections commissioner Orville Pung announced that, pending a successful completion of a three-month work-release program at a Twin Cities halfway house, Thompson would be paroled on March 15, 1983. The action was unanimously recommended by a five-person panel of corrections officials, who determined that nineteen years in prison would be sufficient punishment for the murder of Carol Thompson. The inmate had been a cooperative member of the prison population, Pung said, and would pose no risk on the outside.

Once again the Thompson case was at the top of the local news. The dailies in both St. Paul and Minneapolis ran banner headlines—"T. Eugene To Leave Prison"; "Tearful Thompson Told He'll Be Free"—on their front pages. The papers published long histories of the case and several instantly familiar images: the smiling victim in her cat's-eye glasses, her self-assured, crew-cut husband, several members of the large supporting cast (including Anderson, Mastrian, Segell, Detective Williams, and the six-man, six-woman jury), and an exterior of 1720 Hillcrest looking dark and forbidding against a glum winter sky. In the *Pioneer Press*, there was a photo, dated March 27, 1948, of Cotton and Carol as newlyweds—her gloved hand in his, grasping a large knife, ceremonially cutting their wedding cake—and a crime-lab shot of the family's blood-spattered front hallway almost exactly fifteen years later.

The stories acknowledged the criticism that would surely follow the parole announcement—which it did, mainly and most visibly in the form of irate letters to the editor over the next several days—but the only negative expression recorded in the papers that day was a brief and typically understated response from Otto Swoboda. "My idea is that no justice could ever be done for what he did," Carol's father told the *Dispatch*. "What happens now is nothing I have any control over." Thompson himself was unavailable for comment. A prison official described him as "very thankful and somewhat emotional."

Three of the four Thompson children were quoted in the papers. Patricia, who was then living in West St. Paul, told the *Pioneer Press* that her father should have been released the first time he was eligible for parole, two years earlier. She added that she and her siblings felt that they had been cheated out of both parents, but that the siblings had remained "close" over the intervening years and "nurtured" each other. "We did okay." Somewhat more ambiguously, Patty told the *Star and Tribune* (the Minneapolis papers had merged in 1982) that while she had "basically believed" that her father was innocent of her mother's murder, "that's irrelevant now and that, thankfully, doesn't affect my relationship with my brother and sisters." Amy, living in Louisiana, was her usual direct self, publicly expressing for the first time her opinion about her father's role in her mother's murder. "I think he's guilty, but twenty years is long enough," she said. Margaret either could not be reached or declined to comment.

Jeff had by that time thoroughly reviewed the trial transcript and newspaper clips from 1963. No doubt as a result, he sounded less ambiguous about his father's culpability than he had during the Black interview almost two years earlier, saying he had "finally made peace with the issues." Speaking by phone from Winona, he told the *Star and Tribune*, "I finally felt like I could live with the verdict a year ago after reading all the transcripts and thinking it all out, and I don't have any quarrel [with the guilty verdict]. . . . There's enough evidence, enough circumstantial evidence, for me to believe what happened." However, he added, "Twenty years in prison is long enough. It's just long enough. . . . I guess I'm just grateful we can resume some normalcy, again."

Your Way and Ours

1.

There was no coming-out party, no joyful reunion, no ceremonial salving of old wounds, following T. Eugene's parole in March 1983. Each of the siblings had his or her own family to occupy time and attention, and the three oldest had challenging, time-consuming careers—in other words, busy, separate, and independent lives. There was also, of course, a physical distance between them, with Jeff, in Winona, a two-and-a-half-hour drive from the Twin Cities, and Amy, in Shreveport, a two-hour flight away. T. Eugene, after graduating from the three-month work-release program mandated by his parole, settled into a modest condominium in the St. Paul suburb of Roseville. In fact, only *his* routine seemed to change following his release.

For the children, not having to deal with T. Eugene in prison was an enormous relief. "It's a huge emotional burden for a child—even a grown child—to have a parent in prison," Jeff said later, attempting to explain the siblings' enthusiastic public responses to their father's parole. "We were, frankly, excited by the idea that we wouldn't have to go back there to visit him." There was also, Jeff conceded, the sheer force of T. Eugene's personality, even—or, perhaps, especially—when he was behind bars. Always a skilled manipulator, T. Eugene played on the siblings' conflicted feelings of pity, shame, and guilt, constantly saying, according to Jeff, "I want you to support me on this," "I want you to write a letter for me," and "You're with me on this, aren't you?" Whatever his children had thought about his culpability in their mother's death, T. Eugene had held at least the three oldest siblings in his paternal grip for twenty years. Now, no longer the pitiable, imploring inmate, his emotional leverage was significantly diminished.

Out of prison, T. Eugene was as ambiguous a figure as ever. Now in his middle fifties, he was a pariah, his name synonymous with murder-for-hire in his home state. Legally, he was in a peculiar limbo, on indefinite parole, meaning that as long as the state corrections authority said he was on parole, he was on parole, which, very possibly, would be for the rest of his life. Disbarred as a convicted felon, he could no longer practice law, nor, practically speaking, could he ever expect to teach it, either. He had no career, no viable corporate or institutional connections outside the prison system, and few, if any, realistic prospects. The congenial circle of bridge-playing, concert-going, dinner-partying friends he had once shared with Carol—and who, at least until his arrest in June 1963, professed a belief in his innocence—avoided him. Even the once reliable Doug Young, who had occasionally visited in prison, kept his distance after T. Eugene's release. The house that T. Eugene lived in before and for nearly a year after Carol's murder had long since become the property of strangers. And the one man who could have propped him up and provided him with a liveli-hood—Otto Swoboda—could not bear to speak his name.

Still, the parolee was rarely alone. He had a handful of new friends, most of whom, such as the college professor Dwight Cul-ver and Culver's wife, Margaret, he had acquired while in prison. He still knew how to have a good time, and he retained, despite the physical depredations of middle age and his widespread notoriety, an uncanny appeal to attractive, often much younger women, in-cluding at least one striking law student who surely knew about his past. For a time, during the middle 1980s, his name was linked with that of a local supermarket heiress, though, whatever their re-lationship, nothing apparently came of it.

He did get a job, not long after his release, as a systems analyst with a locally based electronics-store chain. But he was unem-ployed again when the company folded in 1985.

Two years later, in what was billed as his first public appearance since his trial almost twenty-five years earlier, Thompson ad-dressed the Minnesota Press Club in downtown Minneapolis. Wisecracking one moment and serious the next, he told about three dozen bemused listeners that he would appreciate their help in persuading state corrections officials to release him from his open-ended parole. As a parolee, he explained, he could not leave the state without permission and, as a result, had been forced to turn down a job opportunity in England. After the bankruptcy of the electronics firm ("Something about my association," he quipped), his job hunting in Minnesota had been futile. "I paid a fair and reasonable penalty . . . and I think I should now be allowed to begin a new life," he said. Besides his computer skills and sys-tems experience, he said he was licensed to sell real estate. He said he would appreciate any referrals the assembled journalists would care to send his way.

Thompson may not have received any business leads that day,

but he did manage, somehow, to stay afloat. Indeed, he drove a late-model Cadillac, dressed nicely if not as flamboyantly as he had twenty years earlier, and often showed up at local bars and supper clubs with a pretty woman on his arm. After his employment with the electronics chain, he did not, to his children's knowledge, hold a regular job. When asked about his livelihood, he would reply vaguely, or with a joke, about unspecified "deals." Occasionally, he spoke of stock-market successes, again without going into meaningful detail. Years later, his children could only shake their heads and shrug when talking about the source of his unextravagant yet obviously accommodating income.

T. Eugene's relationship with his children was more problematic. "He wanted us to have a normal family relationship, with him as the head of the family," Jeff said. And why not, the older man was prepared to argue. He had not murdered their mother, nor hired anyone else to do it, either—yet because he loved and respected the law, he had accepted the state's incorrect and unjust ruling, manfully relinquished almost twenty years of his life, and now had returned to his hometown to regain what was rightfully his. He was still their father, and now the grandfather of their children. He loved them, as he always had, and expected to be loved in return.

Unfortunately for him, his kids were no longer children. They were grown-ups with their own lives and, more to the point, grown-up convictions about his involvement in their mother's death. Further complicating his case was the fact that his children, with the sensibility that comes with age and experience, had been reviewing his role in their lives before the murder. When they got together for the holidays and on other occasions, the siblings compared memories and addressed questions that, for one reason or another, they had avoided discussing until then.

The particulars of their memories would often diverge and

sometimes contradict each other's, but the siblings agreed that theirs had never been the happy home a lot of people might have thought it was. Cotton and Carol were not the perpetual honeymooners described by relatives and friends after the murder. Cotton was often away from the house, and when he was home, he and Carol often fought. Not with their fists or with flying tableware, at least not so far as the kids could remember, but loudly, and angrily enough. (They laughed and joked with each other as well, which doubtless added to the siblings' confusion.) Carol had quirks and faults of her own. Her children recalled her mishaps with the car. "She was always running out of gas," Margaret said, laughing. "And trees had a way of jumping out and hitting the car when she was driving." They also remembered Carol sometimes departing the house in the middle of the day without announcement or explanation, leaving the kids to fend for themselves until she returned an hour or two later. There was nothing mean-spirited or even willfully neglectful about her behavior, according to her middle-aged children; they attributed the clumsiness and unexplained absences to a certain dreamy absentmindedness. "She could be a ditz, an airhead," Margaret explained, not unkindly, using terms that would have been unknown to her mother in the early 1960s. By contrast, they agreed, their father's behavior was often malicious. They recalled that he seemed to enjoy provoking arguments, not only with his wife, but among the kids. He was, or pretended to be, a principled perfectionist against whose lofty standards they could never measure up. He established strict rules for their behavior, and, in his mind, those rules were always transgressed.

Everybody felt his sarcasm and wrath, but Jeff was continually singled out, the children recalled. T. Eugene criticized the boy mercilessly, for everything from the way he mowed the lawn to his pudgy appearance, his fondness for comic books, and his lackluster grades. When Jeff lost his baseball glove, T. Eugene refused to buy him another one, loudly citing the boy's carelessness. At the dinner table, T. Eugene would order Jeff to stand and spell difficult words according to a fussy protocol, and to repeat the words according to that protocol until his father was satisfied or grew bored. Sometimes T. Eugene would demand that the two of them get down on the floor and wrestle, and then T. Eugene would promptly get the best of the boy and kneel triumphantly on his shoulders. "He was playing around, but not *really* playing around," Jeff said later. Patricia described the household prior to their mother's death as "often a very tense place." And the siblings blamed that state of affairs on their father.

Twenty years later, with varying degrees of enthusiasm, the three siblings who lived in Minnesota acknowledged T. Eugene as their father, expressed their relief that he was out of prison, and told him that they loved him. At the same time, they made it clear where their loyalties lay. Holidays, birthdays, and other special occasions were spent with the Swobodas, who would have nothing to do with T. Eugene. To the best of the siblings' knowledge, the only meeting between Otto and their father after December 6, 1963, took place, quite by accident, in May 1983, when the two men bumped into each other while visiting Margaret, John, and the Wilsons' newborn son, at Fairview Hospital in Edina. According to Margaret, Otto glared at his former son-in-law when the latter arrived with a present for the baby, then left without a word.

T. Eugene stayed in touch, however, calling the kids to exchange pleasantries, sending them greeting cards, occasionally showing up at one or another's house, and once in a while taking them out for dinner. He was an attentive and playful grandfather, and, when he chose to be, a lively and witty companion for the adults. But he was, his children were not surprised to discover, as manipulative as ever, fond, it seemed, of playing one of them against another—"making mischief," Jeff called it. "T. Eugene is a unique person," Jeff once remarked. "He's just him. He can be unbelievably charming and fun to be with and make you feel so proud. He'll tell you how smart you are and how good you look, and you'll believe it and like hearing it, even when you know there's an ulterior motive."

"He was, and is, a very controlling person," Patricia explained. "We weren't used to that for a long time. He didn't have that control when Grandpa was taking care of us all those years. When we were kids, he would say, 'You will do what I say because I'm your father!' But all that time he was gone our grandparents were teaching us to be independent and to think for ourselves. Still, Dad would try to exert his will over us. I was a mother myself by the time he got out of prison, yet he would try to tell me how to dress and what to say."

Once he got out of prison, Patty added, "the issue for us was not so much his guilt or innocence in 1963 as how he would relate to us now, as our father and the grandfather of our kids, all these years later."

2.

But their father's guilt was an issue after he returned home. However firm their convictions by the time he was paroled, his ongoing presence among them and their families eventually led Patricia and Margaret to think again about the terrible events of 1963 and his role in them. (Amy was still living in Louisiana, and keeping her distance, emotionally as well as geographically, from her father.)

T. Eugene never tired of reprising the tales he had been telling since his prison days—about how he had been falsely accused and convicted of a crime he did not commit—and he would re-enumerate, in tedious detail, the "facts" about the homicidal burglars or, in some tellings, the Mafia hit man or men who killed Carol as a warning or payback. The arguments had the mustiness of family apocrypha by that time, and T. Eugene never offered any names or information his daughters had not already heard. Still, he could be persuasive. He could insinuate in a fair-minded person the irrefutable notion, suggested twenty-five years earlier by Hy Segell, that a man's failures as a husband and father did not mean he was a murderer. In Jeff's words, T. Eugene "knew how to hit the right buttons." And, of course, it was one thing to hear such talk from a resident of the state prison—where, as Jeff noted, everyone claims to be innocent—and quite another from a winsome, silver-haired grandfather sitting on the front porch, dandling your child on his knee.

Almost three years had passed when Jeff—the only one of the siblings to have read the 2,400-page trial transcript—decided to clarify the muddled situation. At the time he was working through his difficult decision to switch back from criminal defense to prosecution; perhaps not coincidentally, he proposed a second "trial" for his dad. He would give T. Eugene another chance to prove his innocence to the family. "The ground rules are simple," he explained to his sisters. "Because a jury of his peers has already found him guilty, he will not be presumed innocent. But he can bring any sort of evidence he wishes—any witness, for that matter—and we will give him the opportunity to show us he didn't do it." To his father, Jeff said, "If you want to have a relationship with us, you have to get past this first."

"I wanted to confront him in front of Patty and Margaret," Jeff said later. "He had created doubts in their minds, and they were kind of shaky in their opinions. If he was going to clear himself, he was going to have to do it there and then. He wasn't going to be able to bullshit us any longer. He wasn't going to be able to say, 'Well, I'm your father, and you have to believe what I say.' I told him, 'That's water under the bridge, T. Let's get down to the facts. If you didn't do it, *prove* it.'"

To everyone's surprise—and to no one's—T. Eugene agreed to the challenge.

3.

Unlike T. Eugene's trial in Hennepin County District Court, the proceedings that his son convened at seven o'clock in the evening on January 24, 1986, in the downstairs rec room of Margaret Wilson's south Minneapolis home were a decidedly informal affair.

There were no officers of the court, or spectators, or members of the media present that cold Friday night, though a follower of the Thompson saga could easily imagine the relish with which a Don Giese or Barbara Flanagan would have followed every word with notepad and pencil. There were only Margaret and husband John, Patricia, Jeff, and T. Eugene, who arrived alone and carried only his briefcase. John offered to set up a tape recorder to document the proceedings, but T. Eugene rejected the idea. T. Eugene did, however, insist on taking a few snapshots before they started— "as if this was a long-awaited reunion," Jeff later noted. In what Jeff would remember as an "icily social" environment, Margaret served soft drinks, coffee, cheese, and crackers.

The first order of business was a letter from Amy (who was also in telephone contact from Shreveport), which John read into the evening's record. In a ten-page, handwritten declaration, Amy said, in effect, that while she was convinced that their father had arranged their mother's murder, she believed that he had done his time and, under society's rules, was "due a second chance." What mattered most to her was "the man himself," before and after the murder. She then recounted her fear of him and her "hurt feelings" at the way he picked on Jeff and generally "terrified" the household when they were kids. She talked about the fiction that her father had been hospitalized when in fact he was in prison, and her realization of where he really was, then her fantasies about his innocence, followed by her disappointment when she understood that he was the same man who had made her and her siblings so unhappy when he lived at home. Finally, she wrote, "What I would like is for T. Eugene to understand why he is not 'family.' And why he shouldn't expect to be.... To be quite honest, I doubt if T. Eugene even wants us for a family, but he does need us, doesn't he? He thinks if we accept him wholeheartedly, so will society. He might even get back in the bar if we believe in him. Well, that's his fantasy, kids.

"All I want to say to T. Eugene is take your second chance and go have a happy, healthy life with someone else. 'Cuz the only 'daddy' I claim is Otto Swoboda."

What T. Eugene, sitting poker-faced on the Wilsons' sofa, might have felt as he listened to his youngest daughter's words, he did not say. At any rate, Amy's were only the first of the bitter sentiments expressed that night. Margaret spoke next, emotionally venting her anger at her father for the trauma in the family's home before and after the murder. Patty, who had always been the most supportive of her dad, and the last of the siblings to agree that he was responsible for their mother's death, said only a few words, generally, though in somewhat milder terms, echoing the others.

Then Jeff, seated in a large chair opposite his father, began asking questions. By this point in his career, Jeff had practiced law for ten years, which was, he could not resist reminding his father later, "more years than you ever had [in court], isn't it?" A month earlier, Jeff had decided to return to prosecution after seven years of criminal defense and divorce cases, and he would start work with the Winona County attorney's office in a week. "I wanted to prosecute, in part, because I had resolved my uncertainty about your guilt," he told T. Eugene.

The basic facts of the case, as they were laid out in the transcript and appellate briefs and reinforced by Jeff's own research and courtroom experience over the previous several years, seemed beyond debate. T. Eugene had repeatedly cheated on Carol. T. Eugene had insured Carol for almost $1.1 million. T. Eugene had planned Carol's murder in order to enjoy at least one other woman and live a life of ease and pleasure on the payout from the insurance policies. But T. Eugene had counted on Norman Mastrian to kill his wife. Mastrian was a killer. In fact, it was probably T. Eugene's knowledge of Mastrian's involvement in the Eddie James murder that provided the leverage he believed he had over the tough guy. (T. Eugene may have possessed the gun used in the James killing. Jeff learned that a pistol had been found in one of his father's briefcases after Carol's murder, but, apparently because it had not been involved in the murder, the weapon was mentioned only in passing in police reports.) "T. Eugene believed he had Mastrian behind the eight ball and that Mastrian would never be able to rat on him," Jeff explained later. "Unfortunately for T. Eugene, even Norman Mastrian couldn't bring himself to murder a churchgoing mother of four, so, without telling T. Eugene, he decided to subcontract the job and started auditioning other dirtballs." Thus, when T. Eugene received the news of the attack, he was profoundly shocked, albeit for different reasons than the rest of Carol's family and friends were. It had been, in T. Eugene's mind, a brilliant and foolproof plan by which a murder would look like an accidental drowning. But, Jeff said, Mastrian could not go through with the plan, Carol had been brutally murdered by a hapless "subcontractor," and T. Eugene's scheme had become a disaster.

Jeff believed that the police had done their job and also been lucky, and that Bill Randall's prosecution was patently effective. If the investigation and trial had happened three years later, he thought, the U.S. Supreme Court's landmark Miranda ruling might have made a difference in the roles played by Dick Anderson and other witnesses for the prosecution. An earlier high court decision, *Mapp v. Ohio* (1961), which made the Fourth Amendment regarding search and seizure applicable to the states, was the basis of at least one of T. Eugene's appeals, but made no difference to the outcome. Meanwhile, the accumulation of circumstantial evidence—the insurance purchases, the philandering, the removal of the dog and extension phone—and Anderson's graphic testimony had combined to make, in Jeff's mind, a powerful case against his father.

Yet, from Jeff's highly subjective perspective, the real key to establishing his father's guilt was his father's own words. That meant that T. Eugene's big mistake was taking the stand, which he had probably done against his counsel's better judgment. "T. Eugene did everything lawyers tell witnesses *not* to do," Jeff said. "He volunteered information—not just answering the questions, but saying more than he had to. He argued with the prosecutor, and came across as arrogant and superior. When I finally read the transcript, I immediately knew he was lying. He was asked, for instance, about the location of the telephone extension in the house, and he said the phone could be anywhere, which was an absolute lie. That phone, like everything else in our house, had its place. It could not be moved around. It could not be anywhere other than in its rightful place.

"The jury may not have realized that he was lying about those details, but they surely would have been put off by his superior attitude and long-winded explanations." As for himself, Jeff said he had no doubt—and had not had a doubt since he read the transcript—that the jury's verdict was correct.

Now, like Bill Randall more than twenty-two years earlier, and armed with a yellow legal pad bristling with notes he had drawn in large part from those long-ago proceedings, he moved from one link of Randall's evidentiary "chain" to another, sometimes reading aloud from the transcript. At each link, he demanded an explanation from his father.

"Why did you need so much life insurance?"

"If, in fact, you had had premonitions of your wife drowning in a boating accident, why, instead of buying a million dollars' worth of life insurance, didn't you take the more practical step of buying her boating lessons, or getting rid of the boat, or staying away from the lake?"

"Why did you get rid of the dog? You know we loved that dog. If you were concerned about the new carpet, why not simply have the dog trained?"

"What about the other women?" Jeff mentioned Vicky Miller and the "countless others with whom you cheated on your wife."

T. Eugene had nothing new to say in reply to the questions. But, when Jeff asked about the murder itself, his father put a slightly different twist on the familiar explanation. Willard Ingram killed Carol during the foiled burglary, T. Eugene said, but did so in the course of a sexual assault. He claimed, moreover, that he had the proof in his briefcase. As the hours passed, he posited additional variations on the theme, and, more than once, insisted, as he had so often, that the siblings should believe him when he said he was not involved because he was their father.

At this point—it was now about midnight—Jeff dropped a bombshell. He would later call it his "great secret," and if it was not news to his father, it surely was a revelation to his sisters and brother-in-law. "When I testified for you in December of 1963, all nattily dressed and sworn to tell the truth in a case involving the murder of my own mother, I lied," he told T. Eugene with emotion. "I was fourteen years old, and I committed perjury in a first-degree murder trial. That's what I also realized when I read the transcript. I was lying when I testified about the light in the basement, and I knew it. I was trying to help you."

Jeff described how he had been finagled into the deceit. During the Thanksgiving break in the original trial, he had joined his father's family at the Gesche farm near Blue Earth. At one point, T. Eugene's brother, Wallace, took the boy aside and told him that his dad was in trouble for "something he didn't do" and might go to prison if they could not think of something that would help him. Then Wally asked Jeff if he remembered telling his dad about turning off the basement light before going to school on the morning his mom was killed. Wally said T. Eugene had told him that Jeff had mentioned the light during a conversation Jeff had had with T. Eugene that summer.

"Do you remember that?" Wally asked him. "It could be very important."

Jeff did not remember either turning off the basement light or any such conversation during the summer, but, like the rest of the family, he was confused by all the charges and arguments. He was frightened for his father, and willing to do his part to help.

"Oh, yeah, I remember," Jeff told his uncle. "I turned that light off in the basement. The light was on, and Mom asked me go down and turn it off."

"The next thing I knew," Jeff continued, addressing T. Eugene in the Wilsons' rec room, "I was talking to your lawyers about how I should testify in court. 'Just answer the questions asked,' they said. 'Don't volunteer information. Don't argue. Be polite.'" The day he testified, he said, he spit-shined his shoes and put on his s.p.a. uniform. Someone—Doug Young, probably—drove him to the courthouse in Minneapolis. "And then I was ushered into court to testify in your defense. I testified just like the little trooper I must have appeared to be in my uniform. I'll bet you were so proud."

Showing anger for the first time that night, T. Eugene replied that Wallace Thompson was an honorable man and would be appalled by Jeff's statement. The story, he said, must have been concocted after the trial by the Swobodas.

"No, I lied," Jeff insisted, "and I knew I was lying. Wally is an honorable man, but that's what happened."

In the hush that followed, it was up to T. Eugene to present proof that he had had nothing to do with Carol's murder. He pulled a single document out of his briefcase and said that it established beyond a doubt that another person—someone in addition to Carol and Dick Anderson—had been in the house the morning of March 6. The document was a photocopy of a twenty-three-year-old report, prepared by police criminalist Theodore Elzerman, dealing with blood spatters found at 1720 Hillcrest the day of the murder. According to T. Eugene, the blood "Type B or O with beta factor deteriorated" mentioned in the report had to have come from a third person—namely, the burglar-turned-attempted-rapist-turned-murderer, Willard Ingram.*

T. Eugene handed the document to Jeff. It was, by that time, well past midnight, and everybody needed a break. Jeff and John took the report upstairs to the Wilsons' bedroom. The two men lit cigarettes and read it from top to bottom.

"What does this mean?" John asked Jeff.

"Nothing," Jeff said. "This doesn't prove a goddamned thing."

All Elzerman was saying, Jeff explained, was that blood spatters found at the scene and attributed to the "suspect" may have contained a "weak beta factor." There was nothing in the report, Jeff said, that pointed to another killer. Nevertheless, Jeff and John read the report several times, just to be sure. "We wanted you to prove us wrong," Jeff later wrote to his dad. "We wanted to give you every chance to be innocent of this terrible crime. We wanted to be the victims of the injustice of the system. But we weren't. You were guilty."

When the exhausted party regrouped downstairs, Jeff repeated

* The blood-sample report and the "third-person" argument had been presented by the defense during Mastrian's trial in 1964.

his judgment on both the blood-sample report and their father's presentation. T. Eugene's single piece of exculpatory "evidence" was worthless, he said.

Uncharacteristically, T. Eugene did not argue the point. He had nothing else to say for himself.

Jeff had nothing more to say.

No one said anything for a while. Then T. Eugene sighed and asked where they went from there.

"You go your way, and we'll go ours," Jeff replied. "When you can admit to us what you have done and ask our forgiveness, we may readdress our relationship. But until that time we don't want you in our lives."

T. Eugene protested, as he had so many times before, that he could not admit to something he had not done.

"So," Jeff said later, "we left it at that."

But what forever after would be referred to by the siblings as the "kitchen court" was not quite over. T. Eugene told his children how much they meant to him, and then drew a sheaf of legal forms from his briefcase. Apparently, he planned to write, or hire someone to write, the "true story" of Carol Thompson's murder. But because Minnesota, like most states by that time, had enacted a so-called "Son of Sam law"* requiring that any profits from such a project go into a fund for its victim or victims, T. Eugene needed his children to waive their right to such claims.

---

* David Berkowitz, a.k.a. "Son of Sam," murdered six persons and wounded several others in a series of shootings that terrorized New York City during the mid-1970s. After his conviction, New York state enacted legislation to prevent him and others who followed from exploiting their crimes and notoriety through autobiographies and other potentially moneymaking schemes. Most of the other states, including Minnesota, followed. The constitutionality of such laws has since been successfully challenged in some states, though Minnesota's version remains intact.

Whether anyone gasped, cursed, or laughed out loud at T. Eugene's audacity was not recorded or remembered. But no one signed the waivers.

T. Eugene packed up and got ready to leave. Then, after saying what seemed to be a definitive good-bye to his red-eyed children, he casually asked Margaret if she would like to have lunch with him the following week. Reflexively perhaps, Margaret replied that she would.

"*No*, Margaret, you *wouldn't*," Jeff said sharply. And, as it happened, she did not—at least not the following week.

4.

Many years later, Jeff looked back on that evening as a "miserable experience," but one in which he had done what he felt he must do. He was satisfied, moreover, that he had "argued a strong case based on the [trial] transcript, and confronted my dad with the stories he told, and gave him the opportunity to clear himself with his children." Of course, T. Eugene had not made the most of the opportunity.

"I think it helped the girls," Jeff said. "It gave them the chance to confront T. Eugene with the facts, to see and hear him on the hot seat, to listen to his explanations when they weren't just one on one with him and he could sway them with the force of his personality. It also helped our relationship. They saw that their brother was ready to stand up for them, that I wasn't going to let them be manipulated by their father, that I would protect them from him. So that evening was for the girls. And for me.

"For years, I was very confused about the murder," he went on. "Nothing made much sense to me—nothing about either the crime or life in general. Then I finally realized that my father was guilty. There wasn't a sudden shock of recognition. There were just a few things that hit me—such as his reference to the telephone extension in his testimony. Then, when I read my own testimony and re- alized what I had done.... Well, not that everything fell neatly into place, but it all began to make some sense."

Yet not even the voluminous court transcript, related docu- ments, his own experience, or common sense could satisfactorily answer many of the *why*'s of the Thompson case. Those questions may trouble Jeff, his sisters, and everyone close to the case for the rest of their lives.

Setting aside the obvious moral issues, for example, why would a man of their father's considerable intelligence, material com- forts, professional status, and prospects risk everything on such a scheme? Why, in Jeff's words, would he be willing to "kill the goose that laid the golden eggs"? The siblings, of course, had their own ideas, but they knew that, absent a full admission and ex- planation from their father, those ideas would never put the ques- tions to rest. "You couldn't wait. You wanted it all right now so you killed your wife," Jeff said in the 1996 letter to his dad. Patri- cia and Margaret have suspected that their mother—fed up with her husband's infidelity and perhaps herself involved with an- other person ("Big Red"?)—was preparing to leave T. Eugene. Such a prospect, they believed, would have been unbearable for a man with their father's ego and status-consciousness. Or what if, as Jeff has occasionally wondered, the "Mob" was somehow in- volved, not necessarily as the killers but as the reason for the killing? T. Eugene had been known to gamble with large sums of money and was said to have had contacts with underworld types he met through his mentor, Jerry Hoffman. What if T. Eugene, af- ter a run of bad luck at Las Vegas's blackjack tables, found him- self deep in hock to mobsters? Suppose he needed a large amount of money, and, having bought a year's time from his "creditors," came up with the murder-for-insurance-money scheme?

Jeff even considered the more mundane possibility that his dad had fallen prey to simple envy and the clichéd middle-class fear of lagging behind the Joneses. A few of T. Eugene's associates at the time had become paper millionaires when a couple of Minnesota technology companies took the over-the-counter market by storm—*after* a skeptical or, more likely, impatient T. Eugene divested himself of the stock. "He's almost thirty-five years old, and now he has to find another way to keep pace with his buddies," Jeff suggested. But, expressing that theory out loud, Jeff was neither convincing nor convinced.

Neither Jeff, nor his sisters, nor any of the documents they reviewed had definitive explanations for the several especially curious aspects of the case that perhaps no one could explain for certain, then or ever.

What exactly occurred, for instance, on Tuesday, March 5? Did T. Eugene call home at the appointed time that morning? He had his secretary place the call on March 6 and presumably would have had her place it the day before to trigger the attack and reinforce his alibi. But though Kathleen Zajacz told police that T. Eugene had come in early on the fifth, it was not clear who, if anyone, called Carol at twenty-five minutes after eight that morning. T. Eugene could not have known until later in the day that Mastrian had subcontracted the hit and that the hit man had stayed in bed. Jeff, for his part, had no recollection of his father rising early on the fifth, nor of T. Eugene asking him to latch the front-door safety chain and offering him a ride to school. Decades later, all Jeff would remember of *that* day was the destruction of his comic-book collection and the ugly fight with his mother.

Why had T. Eugene decided on the kitchen phone at the top of the basement stairs as the site of the assault? Had he forgotten that the phone had a long, accordion-style cord that allowed Carol to wander around the kitchen and even into the dining and living rooms while she talked? Why would he assume that she would be standing where the killer could surprise her when he emerged at the top of the basement stairs?

How was Anderson—by his own testimony heavily medicated with vodka and amphetamines—able to function as well as he did on March 6? Granted, he botched the job, but how, given his recent consumption of alcohol and drugs, had he managed to find his way across town to the house and enter it as stealthily and apparently unerringly as he did? After the attack, what were the odds of his stepping out the Thompsons' front door and walking unseen in broad daylight up the block only a moment or two after Carol's flight to the Nelsons'? Would not the Pearsons, having spotted their bloodied neighbor struggling in the snow across the street, have noticed a blood-spattered stranger passing by on the sidewalk seconds later? It is not inconceivable that Dr. Pearson, hurrying across the street to the Nelsons', could have literally crossed paths with Carol's assailant. Yet police documents included no reports of any such sightings or encounters in the wake of the assault.

And how to come to grips with the idea of a woman so modest, or so conditioned by her upbringing and by the conventions of the time, that she returned to her bedroom to put on a robe before running down the stairs toward the door, away from her attacker? Perhaps most chilling of all: How to live with the vision of a husband climbing into bed, perhaps kissing his wife good night, perhaps telling her that he loved her, then falling asleep with the knowledge that when he woke the next morning her murderer would be waiting in the basement—in fact, doing so *twice,* first on March 5 and then again on the sixth? Breakfasting on the bacon and eggs his wife had prepared for him and his children that morning, did he picture her killer crouching in his lair directly below them? If it is possible to believe the reports about T. Eugene's nightmares prior to the murder—that is, to believe that his complaints of nightmares were not part of a ploy to allay suspicion—maybe it is possible to believe that somewhere in his consciousness the prospect of such an event truly rattled him.

As for why it had taken so long for Jeff to confront his father—Jeff was, after all, in his early thirties by the time he thoroughly read the trial transcript—he did have an explanation that made sense, at least to himself.

"Why would I want to reach that point before I really had to?" he asked rhetorically. "There was just this horrible, dark reality in my life. In *our* lives. Nobody in the family had really talked about it up to that point, because, I guess, everybody—at least the adults—knew where everybody stood. As far as my grandparents were concerned, T. Eugene was guilty and dead. T. Eugene's family, meanwhile, insisted that his conviction was a terrible mistake and wouldn't discuss it with us kids. And, all around us, people kept reminding us that our father was a murderer and hinting that maybe we had the same impulses and inclinations that he had.

"I was just a normal schmo trying to work my way through life. I didn't want to sit down and think the whole thing through. I had other problems to worry about, my own life to live. The truth is, I spent a great deal of time and effort trying to ignore the whole situation. Then, one day, ignoring it wasn't an option."

There was, of course, the possibility that if he could not explain away the guilty verdict that January night, T. Eugene would admit his guilt and ask for his family's forgiveness. "If that had happened," Jeff said, "we would have asked why. 'Why did you do such a thing? How could you possibly live with it for so long?' All the obvious questions. But we all knew that it wasn't going to happen. We all knew that it wasn't even a possibility. He's never going to admit it. He can't.

"I don't know if he really believes he's not guilty. I've thought about that a lot. I think he thinks the situation was a lot more complicated than I thought it was, that he's made some mistakes but that he's really not the evil person people think he is. I don't know. I can't believe that he really believes he didn't do it. But maybe he does.

"Could I have accepted an admission and apology after so many years of lies and prevarication? I don't know. We'll never know because it's never going to happen."

Whether anyone at the Wilsons' home that night would acknowledge it or not, T. Eugene's second guilty verdict did not mean the end of their relationship. In fact, only Amy among the siblings consistently kept their father at arm's length over the years that followed the family court. After her husband died, of a stroke, in 1992, Amy returned to the Twin Cities from Louisiana and took a job managing a convenience store. Every once in a while T. Eugene would come in to buy gas for his Cadillac and say hello. Amy was cordial, but did not encourage the contact. When he showed up at a sibling's home for a birthday or holiday celebration, she usually left, unable to understand why he had been invited. Margaret continued to see him on and off. He would contact her, or vice versa. On one occasion, during her separation from John, she called her father for advice on the sale of the Wilsons' home. "He knew the law and he knew real estate," Margaret explained. "He did some research and told me what I ought to do. It wasn't hard for me to ask him for help." Patricia, too, saw her father on occasion. "He's genuinely friendly and outgoing," she said. "He's witty and intelligent, and has interesting things to say. He can really be quite charming and fun."

And Jeff, steadfast in his belief in his father's guilt, met T. Eugene for lunch or another occasion every so often. On one of Jeff's birthdays, he treated T. Eugene to dinner at the Lexington, a favorite of the older man's in years past. Jeff's explanation for their continuing relationship was at once ineffably complicated and profoundly simple:

"He's my dad."

5.

As it does with all things, time wears away sharp edges and obstructions.

Antonia Swoboda, who had seemed to die once with her daughter and then again when her son-in-law was convicted of her daughter's murder, died a third time in August 1974. "She announced when I got pregnant that she could leave now," Patricia said, and, a couple of months after her first great-granddaughter was born, Toni passed away. Otto lived for another twenty years, occasionally going on trips with his widowed sister-in-law, Helen Zabel. "Grandpa was wonderfully fit and healthy and mentally sharp until a year or two before he died," Margaret said. At the age of eighty-eight, he went into a nursing home. "The last time we saw him conscious," said Margaret, "he kept calling me 'Carol' and John 'Jeff.'"

The deaths of their grandparents made relations somewhat easier between the siblings and their father. So, surely, did the siblings' understandable, if largely unspoken, desire for something approaching a "normal" intergenerational family experience as their own children grew. Forgiveness would be impossible unless and until T. Eugene owned up to his crime and apologized, but there could be some qualified acceptance of the man without ignoring his role in their fractured history. A détente was never discussed and agreed upon. It simply happened.

Everybody went about their lives. Patricia called herself Tricia, taught in the Minneapolis public school system, and married Tom Wilson (no relation to Margaret's husband, John), a Vietnam veteran from southern California who worked as a journalist and writer. Margaret had changed jobs and moved upward through the information-systems section of The St. Paul Companies, the giant hometown-based insurer. And Amy, pleased to be close once more to her siblings, eventually went to work at a local State Farm insurance office.

"I think we all evolved and healed and found ways to deal with our situation," Tricia said. "Mine and Margaret's was more of a spiritual path, Jeff's and Amy's, I would say, were along more practical lines."

In 1989, almost four years after prosecuting his father in the family court, Jeff became county attorney—chief prosecutor—of Rice County, an hour south of the Twin Cities. In what may have seemed to some an almost cosmic symmetry, Jeff began doing to others what William Randall, as Ramsey County attorney two and a half decades earlier, had done to T. Eugene. Jeff was now forty years old, a trial lawyer with thirteen years of courtroom experience, the husband of his third wife, the father of three sons, and the oldest child of the state's most famous murder victim and convicted murderer. When he initially applied for the Rice County post, and during two subsequent election campaigns, he liked to say that by virtue of his background and experience, he brought a "unique perspective" to the criminal justice system. No one who knew his story could argue the point. To help combat stress, he began studying tai chi, the ancient Chinese martial art. He drove a white Chrysler with vanity plates that spelled BOOK M, and, at his Faribault office, he and his small staff of young assistants adopted as their theme song the Bobby Fuller hit from the sixties, "I Fought the Law (and the Law Won)." When the pressures of the job and his personal history bore down on him, he steeled himself with a quote from Friedrich Nietzsche: "That which does not kill me makes me stronger."

During his nine years as Rice County attorney, Jeff would oversee the prosecution of thieves, robbers, burglars, kidnappers, rapists, child molesters, forgers, drunk drivers, welfare cheats, deer shiners, and other miscreants, and personally try three men and a woman accused of first-degree murder, which he believed was more, during that period, than any other county attorney in Minnesota. On his office wall he hung the framed verdicts of the three first-degree murder cases he had won. "I don't know if I'd call them trophies," he told visitors. "Maybe they're just proof that once in a while the good guys win." He took his job very seriously, worked hard, and put in long hours. He described himself as "committed." Others, including his third wife, said the correct term was "obsessed." One day in 1995, at the beginning of a particularly intense murder trial, she left a note on his pillow saying that she could not live with him any longer and asking him to move out.

If he did not see his sisters as often as he wished, he stayed in touch and kept them informed of what he was doing. His sisters were proud of him. They thought he was courageous and decisive; whether they believed that on some level of consciousness he was seeking justice for their murdered mother and making amends for his long-ago perjury, they were convinced that he was doing God's work. They would have come down to Faribault's old art deco courthouse to watch him in trial if he had invited them, but he never did, and they did not want to risk embarrassing him, or to add to the pressure by showing up without being asked. Their father, however, felt no such constraints. During the first-degree murder trial of a young man named Timothy Chambers in 1997, T. Eugene drove down from the Twin Cities and took a seat in the crowded courtroom gallery. When the trial recessed for lunch, Jeff introduced his colleagues to his dad, who happily shook hands and chatted like the noteworthy person he would surely be in a room full of lawyers. When someone remarked that he must be very proud of his son, the older man beamed and said, "Oh, yes. I certainly am."

It may not have been more than simple vanity, but friends would note that Jeff, perhaps more than most men his age, often adjusted his appearance. A friend having coffee with him two or three times a year could not help but notice the thick hair brushed low over his forehead on one occasion and slicked back the next, or a bristling salt-and-pepper mustache that, by the subsequent visit, had been either expanded into a full beard or shaved off.

"Trying to stay ahead of the sheriff?" the friend once asked.

"Still trying to find myself," Jeff replied with a smile. He did not seem to be joking.

Jeff was aware, of course, why people he met for the first time—particularly people his age and older, who had grown up in Minnesota and had a memory for lurid headlines—looked at him closely, with a glint, or smirk, of recognition. Fortunately, he had been blessed with, or had willfully developed, an extraordinary mental toughness and a dry, spiky wit that both armored him and enabled him to give as good as he got, at least after he was old enough to know he could fight back. In late 1997, for instance, when the subject of his pending re-election came up in conversation, he referred to the three-way race for governor that was shaping up in Minnesota. That race would pit the scions of the state's legendary Democratic Farmer Labor Party politicians—Hubert Humphrey, Walter Mondale, and Orville Freeman—against one another for the DFL nomination. "Maybe *I'll* run for governor," Jeff deadpanned. "Another son of a famous father."

Jeff did not run for governor, but, in the fall of 1998, not long after he was re-elected to a third term as Rice County attorney, he applied for a district court judgeship that had opened in Winona. (In Minnesota, district court judges are usually appointed, then must stand for election if they seek a subsequent, six-year term.) He thought it would suit him to return to the community where he had labored on both sides of the prosecution/defense divide, now in "the august robes of a judge."

When Governor Arne Carlson, on the recommendation of the state's judicial review board, appointed Jeff to the judgeship at the end of December, he said, "Thompson has earned the respect of prosecutors as well as criminal defense lawyers, law enforcement, and members of the community in general." Though he did not say so at the time, Jeff himself was cognizant, yet again, of the full circle described by his history and career. Just as he had served as county attorney—in the same role that his father's prosecutor had played thirty-five years earlier—he would now assume the mantle of a district court judge, the same as Rolf Fosseen's when Fosseen had presided over his father's trial and eventually sentenced his father to life in prison.

Jeff was not, of course, the only one to appreciate the connection. The Associated Press story that ran in the *Minneapolis Star Tribune* on New Year's Eve 1998 appeared beneath the headline, "New District Judge Appointee Is Son of T. Eugene Thompson." But on this occasion the reference was criticized by readers, one of whom wrote, "What happened when Jeffrey Thompson was 14 years old had nothing to do with his appointment." When contacted by the paper for comment, Jeff responded with judicial restraint. "For a long time I have been trying to become something other than T. Eugene's son," he said. "But, frankly, I'm not surprised [by the reference]. It seems to be the way I'm remembered. It's not irrelevant. I've dealt with it. [But] I wish it had not been in the headline."

6.

T. Eugene had apparently decided to stay below the public's radar following his 1987 Press Club appearance, which, he later remarked ruefully, did not go over well with state corrections officials. There were no more petitions or appeals, and many people might have assumed that he was dead or living in another part of the world. But every once in a while his name would appear in the retirement notice or obituary of a local judge, lawyer, or policeman who had, in one way or another, played a role in the long Thompson narrative. Rolf Fosseen, Hy Segell, and Ernie Williams, for instance, all died within about a year of one another in the late 1990s, and in the obituary of each the Thompson case was described as a career landmark.

Inevitably, in almost every high-profile local case in which a middle-class white woman was believed to have died at the hands of her husband, T. Eugene Thompson's name would be invoked. Following the brutal murder of a young Minneapolis woman named Anne Barber Dunlap in 1995, her husband's struggle to collect on a million-dollar life insurance policy raised obvious comparisons with Carol Thompson's murder and its aftermath. (Bradley Dunlap, who remained a suspect in the unsolved case but was never arrested or charged, reached a settlement for an unspecified amount with the Chubb Life Insurance Company in 1998 and left the state.) It seemed that few connections in the postwar Twin Cities were more likely to assure some lasting distinction than an association, however tangential, with the Thompson case.

In June 1996, T. Eugene once more appeared on the front page of the *Pioneer Press*. Through a bureaucratic glitch, he had been summoned to the Ramsey County courthouse for jury duty and briefly impaneled, though, as a parolee, he was ineligible to serve. After the mistake was discovered and he was excused, he sat down at a McDonald's restaurant with a young reporter named Molly

Guthrey. The "silver-haired and bespectacled grandfather . . . looks wiry and strong, has a firm handshake, and has eyes that seem a little sad," Guthrey, who was not alive in 1963, wrote in the next day's paper. "He cries when he talks about his late wife." Thompson took the unexpected opportunity to reassert his innocence. "People still come up to me after all these years," he said. "It just happened. One juror who was not on the panel with me approached me and said, 'You're T. Eugene, aren't you?' And I said, 'Yes, I am.' And he said, 'I never did believe you were guilty.' And I said, 'I really wasn't.'"

But the media appearances were fewer and fewer as Thompson's contemporaries died or moved away. When his name did surface, it sparked vivid memories among those who remained. Former defense attorney William Fallon, only a few years younger than his long-ago client, acknowledged that Thompson's had been the "case of a lifetime." Fallon, who would later serve as chancellor of the Archdiocese of St. Paul and Minneapolis, pointed out that 1963 had been a remarkable year for many reasons, including John Kennedy's assassination, the murder of civil rights leader Medgar Evers, the bombing of the Birmingham, Alabama, church that killed four little girls, and, of course, here at home, the murder of Carol Thompson. "Things were never the same, for any of us," Fallon said decades later. Some of Thompson's contemporaries still wondered why it happened. "Thompson had such a nice life, such a nice deal," Bill Randall, in his eighties and retired from private practice, said, shaking his head. "I guess he just wanted more." Doug Young, also retired, reflected on his erstwhile friend's wasted opportunity. T. Eugene could have been a very wealthy man, Young mused. He had a bright future in the law and perhaps in local politics as well. He might have been a judge. "Gene was always willing to work hard," Young concluded. "He just wanted to start at the top."

Quietly, and unbeknownst to almost everyone except his family, Thompson married, for a second time, in 1985. His new wife, Margaret, was the widow of Dwight Culver, the college professor who had befriended him in prison. Jeff and his sisters found Margaret immediately likable, and her genteel, sweet-tempered presence at their father's side no doubt softened the edginess of the intermittent Thompson family reunions.

Meanwhile, how the old man had come to think of himself within that broken family circle was impossible to say for certain. His public self-assurance aside, he may not have been certain himself. At the bottom of a Thanksgiving greeting he sent to Tricia and Tom Wilson in 1997, he seemed to be trying to cover all the bases, signing the card, "Love, Maggie and Dad, T., Gene, Cotton, Etc."

7.

Throughout T. Eugene's imprisonment and parole, and throughout their children's maturation into parent- and grandparenthood, Carol Thompson remained frozen in time: iconic and unchanged, yet inexorably fading in the memories of the living.

Her name, and sometimes the familiar smiling photo, appeared alongside T. Eugene's in news accounts during the subsequent years; but, almost immediately, certainly within a few weeks of her death, her image was always secondary to his. He was, and would be, the focus of the breaking news, barbershop gossip, and lunchcounter conversation—while she was, in death, already history. Family snapshots, dutifully collected and pasted on black matte paper in glassine sleeves, could only remind loved ones what she had been in her time.

In the archives of the St. Paul Police Department's homicide division, Carol Thompson was a paper ghost. Details of her truncated life and sudden death were preserved in the hundreds of reports, letters, notes, memos, certificates, photographs, and potential pieces of evidence that made up the investigative component of the

Thompson case. There were the dozens of interviews with friends, neighbors, and acquaintances, often recorded in both the extensive longhand notes jotted down by detectives in Highland Park living rooms and their verbatim transcriptions typed up for George Barkley's review. There were the clinical notations of the emergency room doctors, the forensic photographs of her corpse in the hospital's morgue, and the autopsy report in which far more about her physical aspect would be recorded, down to the size and condition of her internal organs, than she would have ever known about herself in life.

There were, in the dusty police files, Carol's half-typed, half-handprinted personal telephone directory and the 1963 appointment calendar that had hung beside the phone in her kitchen, with her tiny, penciled-in notations—"sign up girls Y.M.C.A.," "Brownies," "perm, me, 8 AM," "SUPPER CLUB," "Circus," "CIRCLE!!!"—that indicated a busy homemaker's schedule. March 6 was to have been a particularly hectic day, including as it did "Pats Scouts" and "Jr. Hi supper." (No reference, though, to the knitting class Carol had discussed with Virginia Koutsky on the evening of the fifth.)

The detectives' hurried but unfailingly legible penmanship and the stenographer's blocky typewriter fonts would become quaint relics of an earlier age, and the entire investigation, as represented by its official record, would seem—despite its outcome—depressingly plodding, redundant, and inefficient. Hundreds of lives played some role in the Thompson murder and investigation, as recorded in the police files. Even here, though, despite the fact that her death was the reason for the massive effort, Carol could decades later be almost overlooked and forgotten in the welter of names, dates, places, faces, and accounts.

She remained, of course, the "better half" in the memories of the couple that friends and neighbors chose to hang on to as the years passed. Sometimes those memories were odd, unexpected, and poignantly telling in their specificity. Decades later, for example, Doug Young would remember an offhand remark that Lieutenant Barkley had made to him a few days after the murder. According to Young, the gruff old cop noted almost wistfully that even *his* wife, on *his* modest civil servant's paycheck, had fancier clothes in her closet than Carol, the "wife of a prominent attorney," had in hers. But then, Young recalled, it was Cotton who had to have the fancy stuff. Carol was happy to make her own (and her daughters') dresses.

Among her children, Carol survived in flesh, blood, and memory, not to mention in the snapshots, table settings, and bric-a-brac typically descended from one generation to the next. "Actually," Jeff said, "I don't remember that much tangible about my mother, but every once in a while I'll look at Amy or Margaret or Patty, and I'll see something that will remind me of her." Amy would remember little about her mother except her scent. She would think of her mother whenever she smelled the essence of almond. ("It must have been her hand lotion," Amy said.) Having heard Carol's voice the night of the murder, Amy did not hear it again. "After that," she said, "when I'd talk to her, I knew I was talking to myself."

Patricia and Margaret recalled dreams and premonitions about their mother, and Tricia would claim to have occasional communication with Carol from the "other side." The older daughters liked to speculate about their mother's relationship with "Big Red," whom Margaret would remember as "a beautiful man, a funny guy, with curly hair," though she and her siblings did not learn the man's real name until recently. "When Mom was with Red, she'd laugh and giggle," Margaret said. "I remember thinking she was so happy, so relaxed. As a kid I thought, 'Isn't it great that Mom has such a good friend?'

"Mom and I were very close," Margaret went on. "She confided in me. The day before she died, I went along when she drove Patty to her flute lesson. While we were waiting, Mom said, 'What would you do if I went away?' I remember telling her that she couldn't leave us. We didn't want to be alone with Dad. And she said, 'Well, what if I was gone for just a little while and then I came back?' I think she wanted me to know that she was leaving.

"In my heart I believe that she was planning to leave Dad. Worse than that—and it took me a long time to admit this to my-self—she was planning to leave all of us, at least temporarily. She must have thought that with Grandpa around, we'd be okay, that Grandpa would take care of us. Which he would have. Which he *did*. I do know that she was an unhappy woman at that time. She felt she needed to get out, to get a divorce. Of course, it didn't hap-pen. But I'm sure that that's what she was getting at when she said that to me the day before she died. She was talking about *leaving*. She didn't know she was going to *die*.

"I was very, very angry with her—that she would even think about doing something like that. She could see I was angry and tried to take back what she said. She said everything would be okay. But I took her seriously and was still angry with her the next day when I left for school."

Margaret, in her family's eyes, grew up to most closely resemble her pretty, petite, myopic mother, but, almost from the day Carol died, it was Patricia who was expected to assume their mother's role. "Beginning at the funeral," Tricia recalled, "people came up to me and said, 'Oh, you're so much like your mother!' 'You have to take over for your mother!' And I think I did. Until Margaret had a home of her own, I was always the one who had the dinners and the parties, and then, after Grandma died, I was the one who made sure we got together. It sounds weird, I know, but in many ways, I think my mother's spirit and mine merged."

One day a few years ago, her cousin Connie called, out of the blue, from her home on the East Coast. "We talked for a while, just catching up," Tricia said. "And then, at the end of the conversation, Connie said, 'You're so much like your mother! You sound just like her!'"

Tricia felt a chill run up her spine. Nobody had said that to her in ages.

EPILOGUE
Phoenix

February 12, 1999—Lincoln's birthday—was a historic date for the
Thompson family as well. At three o'clock that afternoon, Jeff
Thompson was sworn in as a judge of the court for Minnesota's
Third Judicial District.

In Winona, the day was bright, blustery, and bitterly cold, with
windchill readings well below zero. In the third-floor courtroom
of the nearly century-and-a-half-old Winona County courthouse,
more than one hundred and fifty guests had assembled for the ceremony, many of them having driven in from distant parts of the
state. The guests included, robed and seated in the courtroom's
jury box, the two current Winona County district judges, a half
dozen judges from other district courts, and Justice Russell Anderson of the Minnesota Supreme Court. In the courtroom's spa-

cious gallery were Jeff's three sons; Tricia and Margaret, their husbands and children; Amy; Diane Madson, whom Jeff would marry in August, and her two children; friends and professional colleagues from Rice and Winona counties, fellow tai chi students from Faribault, and a miscellany of dignitaries and elected officials from around the state.

Seated front and center among the guests was a well-dressed, vigorous-looking man in his early seventies, with a pink face, thick gray hair parted and brushed over like his son's, and large, squarish eye glasses. T. Eugene Thompson had driven down from the Twin Cities; now, waiting for the ceremony to begin, he chatted amiably with daughter Margaret, seated on the other side of the center aisle. When Jeff walked in and strode toward the front of the room, T. Eugene—smiling broadly—rose to his feet, applauding and extending his hand. Smiling himself, and showing no surprise when he spotted the older man, Jeff shook his father's hand before stepping forward to take the oath of office.

For those who knew the family history—surely most of those in the courtroom—it was an extraordinary sight. To all but family and a handful of others who might have met him at a family gathering, the elder Thompson must have seemed a ghost himself. Not a paper ghost like Carol, but a flesh-and-blood specter from another time and place. Some of the guests were doubtless surprised that he was still alive; so many of the principal players in the Thompson saga circa early sixties had died, while others had maintained such low profiles—Norman Mastrian, for example, on parole in the Twin Cities, and Dick Anderson, on parole in the Pacific Northwest—that they were widely presumed to be dead. Now here was T. Eugene, alive and looking quite well, in the same room as his motherless children, celebrating his son's elevation to the heights of the state's criminal justice system.

The ceremony was dignified and succinct. Following the oath, the Honorable Jeffrey Douglas Thompson, wearing the "august robe" of the position, ascended to the courtroom's bench. His predecessor was a large man, and the chair was too low for its new occupant. For a moment, Jeff looked like a self-conscious schoolboy trying to make himself comfortable in an unfamiliar setting—but only for a moment. Quickly settled in and assured, he spoke for fifteen minutes as "the son of a convicted murderer, the son of a murdered woman, who stuck with law school, became a prosecutor, and is now a judge." He recounted the lessons his grandmother had taught him about perseverance and struggling to triumph over adversity, and what he had learned from his study of tai chi regarding the "duality of human nature." "This is an important event for my family," he said. "We have been recognized by this appointment—as symbolized by this appointment, really—as a family that can rise from the ashes of our mother's death and our father's conviction. The appropriate symbol for our family crest would be the phoenix. I think the Thompson children—I *hope* the Thompson children—will all benefit from this honor."

When he finished and declared the ceremony adjourned, the audience rose and gave the judge a long, heartfelt ovation.

That evening, at Judge Thompson's invitation, a slightly smaller but no less enthusiastic crowd gathered in sport shirts and blue jeans at the Black Horse Tavern south of town. The roadhouse was a large, loud, barnlike structure with a stage and a well-worn dance floor. Jeff was again the center of attention, loving every minute of the party and proving himself a congenial host. When a local band began playing enthusiastic covers of Rolling Stones and Credence Clearwater Revival tunes, he and Diane enjoyed the first dance. His sisters and their families—happy to be sharing Jeff's big day—danced, too. T. Eugene showed up an hour after the others and joined the celebration.

Over the next several hours, at the Black Horse and, later, at the motel where many of the out-of-town guests were staying, the Thompsons partied. And, with the possible exception of his son, no one seemed to enjoy himself more than T. Eugene. He was almost constantly on his feet, hugging grandkids, buying drinks, and dancing with anyone who would dance with him. Only Amy, true to form, would have nothing to do with her father. She had offered him only a wan smile and a few words when he arrived, then stayed out of his way. Nevertheless, in that convivial setting, it was possible to understand why women, and many men as well, were attracted to T. Eugene and enjoyed his company. He was gracious and funny, full of flattery and good-natured cajolery. As anyone could plainly see, he was the world-class schmoozer and master manipulator that his children said he was. But he was also, in his own way, a survivor of a grim and tragic tale.

As the party wound down after midnight, T. Eugene approached Jeff near the door. For a few moments, father and son stood eye to eye—physically, two editions of the same man, separated by slightly more than twenty years. The two of them exchanged a few words, smiled at each other, and shook hands. Then the older man, looking tired and, for the first time in twelve hours, every bit his age, said good night. He walked out the door and into the frigid night, en route to his room across the parking lot. The following morning, when his children and grandchildren regrouped for a late breakfast, he had already departed for the Twin Cities.

Three weeks later—it was March 6, the thirty-sixth anniversary of Carol Thompson's murder—Jeff told a friend that he had not been surprised to see his father in Winona. He said, "I would have been surprised if he hadn't been there." Immediately after the ceremony, Jeff said, they had chatted for a moment. "He came up and said something like, 'Well, I thought that was really a nice speech.

I didn't care for the way you dismissed me, but I'm used to that by now.'" Jeff said his dad had told him that he was proud of him.

Jeff was certain that T. Eugene had had a good time at the celebration. Watching him dance and play around with his kids and grandkids, it was not hard to believe that he was happy to be part of the family, at least for one night.

"Maybe he was thinking about what his life could have been like," Jeff mused. He sounded almost—but not quite—sympathetic. "Maybe, for that one moment, he thought, 'This is the way it might have been.'"

ACKNOWLEDGMENTS

I first met Jeff Thompson in November 1997, when I approached him regarding a magazine story I intended to write that would coincide with the thirty-fifth anniversary of his mother's murder.

Jeff's name had come up a year earlier, when a colleague of mine was reporting a story about an unusual first-degree murder case in Rice County, Minnesota. A seventeen-year-old boy had rammed a stolen car into the parked cruiser of a sheriff's deputy, killing the officer. Jeff was Rice County's chief prosecutor at the time and was personally trying the case. Jeff's name and family history meant nothing to my associate—who was fifteen years younger than I and had not grown up in Minnesota—but they surely did to me. I told him what I remembered about the Thompson case, and that happened to be a lot. I was an eighteen-year-old

Minneapolis high school senior on March 6, 1963, and, like countless other Minnesotans old enough to be aware of earthshaking
events at the time, I would remember Carol Thompson's murder
and the subsequent conviction of T. Eugene Thompson for the rest
of my life.

Flashing back to the case—its unlikely victim and nearly as unlikely perpetrator; its shocking violence, all the more shocking because of its familiar, "respectable" domestic venue; and its cast of
real-life characters worthy of Charles Dickens and Chester
Gould—I decided I would write my own story about the Thompsons. And not only about Carol and T. Eugene, but about their children as well. The 6,500-word account, entitled "A Legacy of Murder" and published in *Mpls.St.Paul Magazine* in March 1998, led to
this book.

I wanted to tell a story that, among other things, extended out
from the crime nearly forty years and acknowledged the fact that
a murderer's victims often include more than the person who dies
at the killer's hands. To do this, I had to have the help of many people, most importantly the Thompson children. Telling their story,
I hasten to say, was not their idea, nor was it something they agreed
to help me do without reservations and second thoughts. Years
ago, as young adults, they agreed that they would never attempt to
capitalize on their extraordinary history. Nonetheless, when I told
Jeff and then his sisters what I had in mind, they all eventually
agreed to cooperate. Intelligent, congenial, and generous people,
they answered every question I thought to ask and asked nothing
of me in return. In separate conversations, they spoke at length
and in detail about their individual and collective histories and
what they remembered from 1963. Jeff and I spoke dozens of
times, during long discussions in Faribault, Winona, and the Twin
Cities, and in shorter exchanges via the telephone and e-mail. One
memorable evening, he and I spent a couple of hours exploring

1720 Hillcrest Avenue, in Highland Park—the first time Jeff had been inside his boyhood home since he was fifteen. He and his sisters also included me in family events: birthday parties, career celebrations, their children's graduation open houses. I was especially honored to be present at Jeff's installation as a district court judge and, a few months later, at his marriage to Diane Madson. Whatever their varied reasons for opening their lives to me, I believe the siblings were as curious about their past and their legacy as I was.

Though I have met and spoken several times with T. Eugene Thompson, most often at some of the family gatherings I mentioned above, he has cordially but resolutely refused to talk to me on the record. He was wary, he explained on one occasion, of jeopardizing what faint hope he held out for the state releasing him from his parole. I cannot imagine, in any case, that he would have told me anything he has not already told others countless times— that he had nothing to do with his wife's death—and I cannot imagine that I would have believed him. I did talk, however, to several of his contemporaries; most notable among those willing to speak for attribution were William Randall, William Fallon, and Douglas Young. For their assistance, and for the cooperation of others not named here whose recollections have been important to my attempt to recreate the events of that time and place, I am immensely grateful.

But I am old enough now myself to appreciate the limits and untrustworthiness of memory, so I have relied, for much of the long-ago history recounted in this book, on a wealth of sources from the time of the Thompson murder, investigation, and trial. These include police reports, medical records, trial transcripts, personal correspondence, newspaper and magazine clippings, even snippets of scratchy television-news film that provided—piece by piece and in the aggregate—an often startling immediacy, richness of detail, and veracity not possible via even the most acute hindsight. My account also benefited from the information available in the late Donald John Giese's book, *The Carol Thompson Murder Case*. I doubt that any journalist at the time knew more about the Thompson case than Giese. I first read his nuts-and-bolts review of the crime not long after it was published in 1969, and, thirty years later, I was pleased to rediscover it at a used-book store.

I am indebted, in addition, to a number of living sources, helpers, friends, and family members, including Barbara Flanagan and Jim Klobuchar, venerable Twin Cities newspaper people who wrote about the case and its principals at the time and afterward, and who shared their recollections with me in conversation; my pal Bruce McManus, who, coincidental to our friendship, was one of several wardens of the state prison at Stillwater during T. Eugene's incarceration, and provided information regarding prison life and Minnesota's corrections system at the time; the St. Paul Police Department's former chief William Finney (now retired), former homicide commander John Vomastek (now senior commander in charge of the department's Central District), and former records section sergeant Linda Wilson (now a sergeant in its Western District), for allowing me to sift through and helping me make sense of the voluminous Thompson case files; former St. Paul police spokesperson Officer Paul Schnell, his successor, Sergeant Chris Nelson, and Officers John Morrow and Peter Crum, for answering a miscellany of historical questions; James and Terese Radford, current owners of 1720 Hillcrest, for inviting Jeff and me to visit their home; *Mpls.St.Paul Magazine* editor Brian Anderson and former executive editor Bonnie Blodgett, for the opportunity to tell the Thompson story the first time; my writer friends and colleagues Dick Coffey, Kim Dalros, Paul Froiland, Dobby Gibson, Steve Kaplan, Brad Pecelj, Walter Roers, Bette Sack, William Souder, and Adam Wahlberg, for their interest and ideas; my oldest, dearest buddies, Jack McKeon and Dean Tjosvold, whose camaraderie and counsel I count on; and, most essentially, my wife, Libby, and children, Joe and Katie, for their unstinting love, enthusiasm, and support, and for accommodating my obsession with dark subjects.

I also wish to thank Ann Regan, editor in chief at Borealis Books, for her indispensable judgment, guidance, and belief in my book. Top to bottom, Borealis has been an outstanding partner in this project, so, additionally, my grateful cheers go to director Gregory M. Britton, director of marketing Alison Vandenberg, and design and production manager Will Powers.

I owe my profoundest thanks, though, to Jeffrey Thompson, Patricia Wilson, Margaret Wilson, and Amy Simmons. Whatever they think about the result of my efforts, this is their book as much as it is mine. It is my telling, but their story.

Dial M was designed and set in type at Borealis Books by
Will Powers. The typefaces are Clifford and Franklin Gothic.
Dial M was printed by Maple Press, York, Pennsylvania.

CPSIA information can be obtained
at www.ICGtesting.com
Printed in the USA
JSHW031130281220
10587JS00002B/178